MY TREK WITH DIVINE DESTINY

A MEMOIR BY HORST HEHR
CLINTON, IA 2015

This book is a memoir. Herein, the author has data of people, places, and events based on the best of his memory.

Published by GloriaDei Press

ISBN-10: 0692543252

ISBN-13: 978-0692543252

Cover design by Dionne Witt

Cover art: Insert photo by Jean Hehr, model of covered wagon, (made by Guy Payne, 2015), similar to the one used on the "trek", resting on the hand loomed blanket made by the author's great grandmother. Background photo courtesy of Shutterstock.

Map artist: Jamie Elkins

Foreword

During the course of my adult life, I have had the privilege of hearing the stories of many parishioners, patients, and their families.

At times, I have also had the opportunity to speak with them or others, either individually or in groups, about portions of my own life story. Over and over, following these conversations or presentations, I have been encouraged to write down my own life story, such that these discussions and presentations could be expanded to include additional details. What follows in this book is my attempt to fulfill these requests.

A brief overview of my journey in life may be helpful here. I was born to a devout Christian family in 1938 in Alt-Posttal, Bessarabia, a small Russian village north of the Black Sea. My ancestors and relatives had lived and prospered there and in nearby villages for four generations. They originally came there in response to an 1812 invitation from Tsar Alexander I. Other German migrants had accepted invitations to other parts of Russia from Catherine the Great, Alexander's grandmother, as early as 1763. These invitations were extended to develop the Russian economy. Settlement of the fertile agricultural land in Bessarabia was occasioned by Alexander's acquisition of it in 1812 through treaty agreements with Turkey. More about this history, migration, and the life of my ancestors there may be found in the Appendix.

In October 1940, orders came from Hitler through the German SS that the residents in the area where we were living were to be expelled and deported to Poland so that the areas captured at the start of WW II could be repopulated with German people. An alternative choice to live under Communist rule existed but was rejected by my parents because they believed it would be a Godless society. This forced departure from Alt-Posttal was the first of many times in my young life that our family was to lose virtually all of its possessions to meet circumstances and/or challenges by relocating for survival or our well being. These included, but were not limited to, our flight ahead of the Red Army near the end of WW II and even our eventual immigration to the USA.

The many miles of travel and much time spent in relocation, especially during the war, led to numerous difficulties, many life threatening. Through each difficult situation my family, especially my dear widowed mother, was led by the hand of God or a guardian angel sent to support and protect us. I believe that the verses of Chapter 12 from II Corinthians beginning with 7b well represent our empowerment from God:

"... there was given me a thorn in my flesh, a messenger of Satan, to torment me. Three times I pleaded with the Lord to take it away from me. But he said to me, "My grace is sufficient for you, for my power is made perfect in weakness.""

When prayer is not answered in our lives according to our will or hopes, do we still find sufficiency in God's grace? Must thorns infest our life to make the grace of God more obvious? Is His grace sufficient in all things?

In closing, I give thanks again to God for the many people who kindly assisted us in those difficult days and in my life's journey till now. Most recently my wife, Jean, John Liittschwager, and Ann Lowery have given substantial assistance in proofreading and editing the manuscript of this book and are given my heartfelt thanks for their efforts on my behalf. Thanks also to Judy and Phillip (Skip) Carstensen for proofreading. Thanks also go to my sister, Elmire Rosnow, who so generously shared photographs from her collection for the book. Unless otherwise noted all pictures are from her or my personal collections. And finally, I thank my niece, Dionne Witt, for her gracious help leading to the publication of this document. God be praised!

TABLE OF CONTENTS

Trek Route

1. Tarutino
2. Alt-Posttal
3. Odessa
4. Vienna
5. Torun
6. Berlin
7. Gyhum
8. Bremen

Russia

Bessarabia

Dniester River

Romania

Prut River

Jamie Elkins 2014

Poland

Germany

Vistula River

Russia

Austria

Bessarabia

Romania

Danube River

Black Sea

LEAVING BESSARABIA

My mother told me the German SS troops came to Alt-Posttal on October 4, 1940. On this day my father had released all the livestock to forage on their own and had closed his blacksmith shop. He and my older brother Friedrich, then eight, were loaded into the back of a large truck with other men who had also refused to live under Communist rule and taken away to an unknown destination. He had no choice but to leave behind my mother, my younger sister Elmire, and me, as well as everything that had been developed and worked for by the previous generations.

My mother, too, in her third trimester of pregnancy, was forced to leave their comfortable, familiar home. She traveled alone with Elmire and me. I had just turned two, and Elmire was one. We were all put onto a bus, along with our suitcases. Mother had packed as many cloth diapers as she could (made from torn sheets given by the neighbors), the family Bibles from both sides of the family, baptismal certificates, their marriage certificate, and a wool blanket of red and green on a field of gray, which had been woven by her mother's grandmother and given to her mother and father as a wedding present.

My parents were taken, each separately, unsure of where the truck and bus were going, or if they would ever see each other again. They were going in faith as Abraham did when he was told to leave Haran, not sure what the final destination would be. My parents left with the same confidence of Abraham: they believed that God would lead and provide, that His grace would be sufficient.

Mother reported that after three days, which included travel and being directed and redirected by various organizations, she and Father found each other where the Danube River empties into the Black Sea. Their separation ended, and the family was reunited. Their faith had sustained them. They were then put on a boat that took them up the Danube.

What consisted of many unknowns to my parents were actually very carefully orchestrated plans of the Germans. The German troops systematically moved from town to town, settlement to settlement, forcing the removal of the population from the entire area by early December. A website published by the Odessa Digital Library,* *Evacuation from Bessarabia and Bukovina, 1940,* reports a version through actual documents from that time. The original plan had been to truck the people to ports along the Danube River where they could be loaded onto ships for resettlement. Because of the poor roads, this proved impractical, and the people were taken to nearby rail stations and then transported to the port cities of Kilie, Reni, or Galatz for evacuation. (More than likely my parents, paternal grandparents, and aunts from Alt-Posttal, as well as my maternal grandparents and aunts from Tarutino, were transferred to the rail

2

station at nearby Beresina and then transported to Reni, where they were loaded on ships for the journey up the Danube. It is possible, however, that my family was among those who proved the original transport system impractical, as the documentation I found had the first trains leaving from Beresina on October 8. It is also possible that is not the route they took, and it could be my memory of the dates is also inaccurate.) Under the new plan the many trains from the various areas of Bessarabia ran continuously to the ports, shuttling a thousand at a time. The railways had specified times to load and unload passengers and were fined if they did not meet the designated time allotments. Passengers were responsible for their own bedding, eating utensils, and personal items, the total of which could not exceed 35 kg/person and were to be carried with them. The clothing worn by children under ten years of age was to have the destination code sewn or indelibly marked on each piece so that the child could be reunited with the parents should they get separated. How difficult it must have been for my mother, pregnant and traveling alone with two small children before she met up with my father, to meet these requirements. I can only hope that some of the other women from Alt-Posttal gave her assistance.

*(http://www.odessa3.org/collections/war/link/evac317.txt; www.graumann.us/custom-1/ss_ evacuation_bessarabien_1940.pdf)

Left to right: Elmire, Mother Adele Hehr, Horst, and Friedrich, summer 1940.

Aunt Nelly Tetzlaff Sanwald, sister of Adele Hehr, in front of the Hehr house in Alt-Posttal, Bessarabia, during a visit in 1991. Horst and Elmire were born there. The blacksmith shop is in the rear.

ON TO AUSTRIA AND POLAND

After the concerns of being separated, traveling alone, and finally being reunited, the five-day trip up the Danube River to Vienna seemed relatively uneventful. The only problem was that Father had to leave Mother and us three children each evening, since the men and women were not allowed to overnight together. He helped Mother in all aspects of infant and childcare and then, at the last possible minute, left them to find a place to sleep in the men's section of the boat. Because he stayed with Mother as long as possible, the other men had already selected the best sleeping places by the time he arrived, and he was forced to sleep in a cold, drafty place. The report I received from my mother on this subject was that he had to sleep where there were significant drafts, but compared to all they had already experienced, this was a problem that he would endure.

During the day the boat ride offered interesting scenery with vineyards and castles. At times the interest was great enough to cause many people to move to one side of the boat, and the captain had to request that some people move to the other side lest the boat tip. Passing through the Iron Gate, a very steep incline near the Transylvania Alps, was also quite interesting. To help counter the rapids and assist in making the incline, the boat was hitched to a cog railroad engine, which helped pull the paddlewheel boat up the river past this point.

Once the boat brought our family to Austria, we were assigned to barracks at Schwinteg for two weeks. During this time my father was admitted to the hospital for ailments not yet clear, but indicating kidney problems, ostensibly attributed to the time on the boat when he had to sleep in the drafty conditions. We were then transferred to Lager Bacham, near the Austrian village of Mühldorf in the state of Lower Austria. The barracks, which had been vacated by German soldiers now fighting on one of the various German fronts, became what we thought would be a temporary home for us five, soon to be six, Hehrs; however, it turned out to be longer than we expected.

After being here about two months, Mother gave birth to my younger brother on the second to the last day of 1940. Our parents named him Adolf. After I learned the strange and horrible truth about Adolf Hitler, I inquired of my mother why she would name her son after this wicked dictator. She replied that his name had been planned long before she ever had to deal with the dictator, Hitler. The naming was a pure coincidence.

Though we were to have been placed in Poland after we left Bessarabia in the fall of 1940, it did not happen until nearly a year later. On November 14, 1941, we went north by train into Poland, arriving in Topolno, Kreis Schwetz. Here, as in many other places, the local Polish residents had been forced to leave their homes to make way for the many displaced German families coming from Russia, including mine. How easily Hitler played with the lives of people under his sway.

The little farm assigned to us was on a high place; in fact, we could see the Wisla River, commonly known now as the Vistula. In German it was called the *Weiksel*. A portion of our land actually adjoined the river. Each spring this land would flood because the source of the river far to the south would melt faster than the waters to the north and would overtake the ice and flow onto the land. This area was left for pasture since it was unsuitable for crops due to the flooding.

The transfer of the Poles from their homes and the assignment of these places to incoming refugees took place under the piercing eyes of Nazi party members. My parents were instructed never to eat with the Polish people, even with Vitold and Maria, who had been assigned to help us on the little farm. They were not to be paid and were to be treated as slaves because we Germans were of the "superior" race. My parents responded to the Nazi official who gave the instructions that they would never treat the Poles, or anyone else, in this manner. They reminded the Nazi official that we are all created in the image of God and that we are to love our neighbors as we love ourselves, just as our Savior taught. Their response to the Nazi instruction was courageous and theologically sound. Mother and Father gave our Polish helpers a good salary, had them eat at the table with us, and treated them in the manner Christ would have us treat others.

Mother reported that the officious Nazi giving the instructions had lost his leg in combat, and apparently this fact fostered his inflated opinion of himself. Though his face turned red and he was obviously angry at their reply to his instructions, he said nothing and left abruptly. Mother thought that he realized that this family had three sons, whom Hitler catered to and protected because they would soon do his bidding, and this fact probably took precedence over the insubordination they had shown to him. For this reason, despite his anger, the "welcoming" Nazi did not discipline my parents, as was often the case when Nazi demands were not met.

Left to right: Horst, Elmire, Roman Catholic Sister Resi Wurfbaum holding Adolf, and Friedrich at our temporary quarters at Lager Bacham barracks, Mühldorf, Austria, 1941.

Maria, our Polish domestic helper from Topolno, Poland

Uncle Ernst Tetzlaff, on leave from the armed services, holding Horst and Elmire, at Lager Bacham barracks, Mühldorf, Austria, 1941.

THINGS SUDDENLY CHANGE

So desperate was Hitler for soldiers by 1942 that even though my father was in very poor health and forty years old, the German army conscripted him into military service. He was scheduled to report for duty at the end of September, but that did not happen. He became much sicker, and on October 17, 1942, Father's kidneys failed and he died.

The last month of Father's life became a severe test for all concerned. He developed blindness, became extremely irritable, and chose to decline the medical offer of a nephrectomy, though he had been assured that this surgery would solve most, if not all, of his ailments. His response was a faith response. Should the dear Lord choose to heal him of his kidney problem, so let it be; should He not, the consequences would be taken with good faith.

Perhaps, just perhaps, my father dealt with his intellect and with his emotions regarding his kidney problem in the same manner he had dealt with leaving behind his property and livelihood in Alt-

Posttal. Should the dear Lord choose to remove him and his dear family from all that he and the three previous generations had worked for in Alt-Posttal and which would pass to the next generation, so let it be. In the same manner should the dear Lord choose not to heal him, so let it be. The consequences would be taken in good faith, which Father apparently did. How I wished I had been old enough to discuss this grave and profound subject with him before he died.

Since I was born August 9th, 1938, I was just four years old at the time of my father's death. I did not know nor could I grasp the implications of his decision to remain faithful to God and His beloved Son, Jesus Christ by leaving Alt-Posttal. At my age I could only relate to him as my father, and my memories are those typical of a child. I remember times when his muscular arm and strong left hand would reach out to discipline me because I would balk at eating what was set before me, and I would scoot off the bench and under the table. I also remember he was gentle and caring. I remember him, dressed in his brown hat and a light green shirt and dark green pants, sitting at the end of the driveway one day, keeping the cows from going into the street. It happened that I had slept late and came running out of the house still in my pajamas after discovering that all the cows were foraging in the ditches of the driveway. Father was sitting there keeping watch. The temperature was unusually warm, and I took off the shirt portion of my pajamas and simply dropped it. A very hungry or curious cow decided to taste it and began chewing on it. Father noticed this and called for Vitold, who immediately chased the cow, and it then dropped my pajamas. Despite the damage to my pajama shirt, I recall no discipline from my father, but only reassurances that I was safe, my pajamas were not that important, and a replacement could be made.

On the day of Father's death he was still alert but had been blind for the last four weeks. He asked Mother to get the Bible, find the second chapter of Mark, and read verses 1 through 12 to him. This reading is about a time when huge crowds who wanted to see and be near Jesus enthusiastically followed Him. Some people carried a paralytic on a cot to the house where Jesus was so that Jesus could heal him, but they could not gain access because of the crowds. Getting to Jesus required more than the usual effort because Jesus was inside. To get inside through the crowds was impossible, so they decided to go over them. The friends took their ailing friend to the roof, located the spot where Jesus would be beneath them, and began to remove tiles and whatever was in the way to make a space large enough to let their friend down through so that he might meet Jesus. With great effort this was achieved, and Jesus forgave the sins of the paralytic man. Some there thought Jesus did not have the authority to forgive sins. Jesus proved His authority, His divinity and His humanity, by caring enough to forgive the sins of the paralytic and heal him. He proved that He is who He claims to be and, therefore, is quite able to grant the forgiveness of sins. This is what my father soundly affirmed, according to Mother's report.

Father wanted to hear once more that his sins were forgiven. Shortly thereafter he asked Mother to hitch up the horses to the best wagon so that he could travel – into the arms of His Savior Jesus Christ. It was not horses and wagon but angels and their divine arms that lifted and carried my father to his eternal home. His ailing body was healed with the gift of an eternally whole one. He could now see perfectly. He was free of the pain from his kidney problem, safe from any "ism," and able to worship the Triune God without any hindrances whatsoever. He was in his eternal home. This final ministry of Mother to her beloved husband gave her much strength then and in the years to come.

*   *   *

Upon Father's death, Mother had no funeral home to go to, or even relatives nearby to help her prepare Father's body. A good neighbor and his wife, however, did come to assist in the preparation for burial, which took place on October 22, 1942.

The day before the burial, Father's body was lying in the casket in our front room. During this time of viewing it was customary not to have the legs covered in the casket. My sister, Elmire, and I were alone in the room with Father. Because we were only three and four, we could not see completely into the casket. We pulled over a chair, and both of us climbed on it, holding on for dear life so as not to fall off. We then could see Father in his entirety and that he truly was not moving; he was dead. We began to sob and declared to ourselves and each other that our *"Deide hun no gschtorba."* This was spoken in our first learned language, Schwabisch, a south German form of Low German and meant, "Dad has now died."

Our weeping and grieving was unique in the sense that no adults happened to be in the room with us to tell us children to stop our crying, our grieving. We were left to our God-given means of fully expressing what was deep in our souls, the need to weep, to let the tears wash out at least some of the deep hurts in the loss of someone very dear to us.

I wonder if this experience of freedom in expressing deep and powerful feelings was a special purposeful blessing from God for my later life when I had the privilege of ministering to people in congregations, and still later as a chaplain in the hospitals, to those with similar needs. In Romans 12:15 we are encouraged to "…weep with those who weep," to offer caring support, even with tears at times. Grieving and weeping are quite all right, especially in the hurting times of death in the family. Much later in the United States I learned sayings that prevail in the Western culture on this subject: "Big boys don't cry," and "Suck it up." This attitude avoids the very tools God designed for healing the hurts forced into our lives. Yes, I realize that we do not cry in trivial situations, but I do know that there are times when even big boys do need to cry and times when we do need to let tears wash out our sorrow, anger, and confusion.

My memories from age four were that Father was buried in a cemetery that had a brick pillared, steel gate, and he was buried immediately to the left of the gate. In October of 2003, my wife Jean and I traveled back to Germany to attend the 50th wedding anniversary of my aunt and uncle, Elfriede and Arthur Sonström. We traveled with my cousins Doctors Renate and Norbert Henze to Topolno, Poland, where we were living when my father died. Renate was searching for family heritage, as her father had been resettled into this region as well. I was focused on finding my father's grave. I hoped to find a stone engraved with his name and dates, but none was to be found. We had been told that perhaps two other persons might have subsequently been buried on the same site, since by law a burial spot is retained for only thirty years and, if not repurchased or regularly cared for, is forfeited after that time. We did find an untended grave in the spot I remembered. It had no identification, flowers, or other decorations, but only a steel cross – which we found to be true for many Germans buried during the German occupation of Poland. I was touched by the kindness of the Polish people in allowing burials in their cemeteries of people who had occupied their land, some most rudely.

The priest serving the church where I inquired about Father's grave was not helpful and seemed almost rude. He claimed, via poor communication due to the language barrier, that he had been at this parish only for five or so years and had no knowledge of events back in 1942. Furthermore, he was unwilling to let me see the records of deaths in the parish. We did get a soil sample, which my sister, Elmire, had requested, and pictures of the cemetery. Unfortunately we did not get a picture of what we believe was the gravesite. But I did feel connected once again after 61 years.

My father, Johann Hehr's induction photo, taken months before his death in 1942.

Horst and Jean Hehr in 2003 visiting the cemetery in Topolno, Poland, where Johann Hehr, Horst's father, was buried October, 1942.

Horst in 2003 showing the way to Topolno, where the family lived in 1941 and 1942.

WE MOVE TO RHEINSBERG

Mother, now basically alone after Father's death and having no relatives nearby, applied for a transfer so that we could be closer to her parents, Eduard and Maria Tetzlaff, who lived in Rheinsberg, (*Rynsk* in Polish), Kreis Briesen. Her request and prayers for the transfer were granted, and in the spring of 1943 we left Topolno for Rheinsberg. She was assigned a small farm located across the street from her parents and less than one kilometer from Rheinsberg.

Her assigned helpers again were Poles, Stachek and Agnes. They were delightful people, and we children preferred them for childcare due to their loving kindness and gracious care, especially when Mother had to leave for business purposes. On occasion, Agnes invited us children to bring our little cups to the cow barn while she was milking the cows. She told us to hold our cups at a certain tilt, and then she pressed the teat of the cow and succeeded to fill our cups with truly fresh and tasty warm milk. I still prefer to drink my milk warm.

The small farm consisted of about thirty acres of tillable land, a small orchard, a house/shed combination, a chicken/duck house, a granary, and a barn that housed some pigs, our ten or so cows, and our horses Lise and Lotte. These buildings were placed into a square arrangement with one arm of the square open. That is where the well for drinking water, the *Brunnen*, was located.

Between our house and the street was a beautiful flower garden, and near the fence was a small orchard consisting of cherry, apple and pear trees. My favorite was a cherry tree, and often brother Fritz and I were in the tree enjoying the cherries when Mother was calling us for mealtime. Apparently she did not see us up in the tree and gave up calling. I did have my fill of cherries and, at other times, apples and pears.

Looking from the well toward our small village of Rheinsberg, we could observe a stork family. They had their huge nest at the top of our neighbor's barn. Those buildings were about half a kilometer from our farmstead on the same side of the street. To see those huge birds gliding down toward that nest to feed their little ones was impressive. At times the parent storks would be "grazing" in the pasture located between our farm and theirs. They were a source of significant entertainment for my family and me. In the fall of 1944 before we fled the following January, I remember seeing a bunker being built right next to the barn where the storks nested. I wonder if the storks, which fly south for the winter, returned there and nested in the summer of 1945 or if they were driven away by all the army activity going on just beneath them. In our travels there in 2003, I could not find the barn, the storks, or the bunker.

Mother also had hens hatch some little ducklings, and she took the newly hatched ducklings outside on a sunny spring morning, placing them between the house, the cement steps, and a makeshift fence. My brother apparently noticed that these little golden fluff

18

balls could turn their heads beyond a 45-degree angle. He was curious to learn just how far their heads could turn. Was it 90 or even an additional 45 degrees? Could it be as far as 180 degrees? He decided to experiment by turning a duckling's head to see how far it would go. The little duck became limp. This little fluffy candidate had died, so he tried his scientific experiment on several more until Mother came out of the house, noticed what was happening, and turned his head beyond his comfort zone to make her point.

Behind our barn was our favorite spot, a small pond. How often we children would splash and swim in it. One day we saw a mother hen, having hatched duck eggs, scolding her ducklings for swimming on the pond, where she could not control them. She would run around the pond clucking vehemently, unable, however, to convince the little ducklings to join her on land. My young mind knew ducks are designed for swimming, and I wondered why the mother hen did not understand this.

One winter I recall Mother telling me that she thought the pond was frozen over. When I heard this, I decided to check out her information and began walking on the newly formed ice. As my feet took more steps onto the pond, the ice seemed to sway with them. Somehow I came to realize that the ice was very thin and that at anytime it could break and I would surely sink due to my heavy coat and other water absorbing clothing. No one else was around, and I knew yelling would be fruitless. The realization of how profoundly dangerous this situation was made me very frightened. Desperate prayers for help rose. The help I sought from above came, and the ice held. I learned an important lesson about ice safety and after that asked an adult first whether the particular situation could be managed by me alone or if I needed some help.

When we had done something foolish such as the ice incident, Mother would often sigh with the expression, *"Oh Jerim, Oh Jerim."* I do not know what it means, but it must have meant something comforting to her because her apparent stress level seemed to diminish. How she must have missed my father. Only recently have I learned that this saying may mean, "Oh, that I had tears enough to weep night and day for my loved ones."

Horst in 2003 showing where the family lived from late 1942 to January, 1945. Rynsk was renamed Rheinsberg during the German occupation.

Horst in 2003 on the farm where the family lived in Rheinsberg.

Horst, Adolf and Elmire with domestic helper, Agnes, in Rheinsberg, 1943.

Front: Horst and Elmire. Rear: Mother Adele Hehr, Friedrich, Aunt Nelly Tetzlaff, and Grandmother Elisabeth Tetzlaff at the family home in Rheinsberg. 1944

Mother, Adele Hehr, by the wagon. 1944

Mother, Adele Hehr, transporting soldiers with the horses and wagon. 1944

Horst riding one of Grandfather's horses. Grandfather walking behind.

Grandfather raking hay.

Rynsk Church, where the Hehr and Tetzlaff families worshiped.

THE REALITY OF WAR REACHES ME

Our Polish hired hand, Stachek, used his wonderful wood carving talent to carve an airplane for me. It had propellers that actually turned when the plane was held into the wind. Often I held my precious gift by the corner of our house, where the wind seemed strongest, and delighted in the whirring sound of the two propellers. While enjoying my airplane, I noticed in the sky above quite a few real airplanes. They seemed to be angry at each other and flew against each other, and then one or two would come tumbling down with a lot of black smoke trailing behind them. I ran into the house to inquire from my mother why those airplanes did not fly right. She responded with a cautious voice, "Horst, Hitler is at war with many countries, and those airplanes are a part of the war. Germany's airplanes are fighting off those of the other countries." I could not understand why such nice, real airplanes were being so rudely destroyed.

Each Sunday afternoon a dear friend, Mrs. Mittelstedt, walked from her farm, past our place, into Rheinsberg for Sunday School. By the time she reached us, several children were already gathered at her side. She would stop for us, and then Fritz, Elmire, and I would join her group of eager children walking to the only church in town. This church had been Catholic and was now Lutheran. I recall vividly the very room in the church where we met. It was furnished with dark green benches and had special little songbooks. I still have a copy of the songbook, which I believe I received as a Christmas gift. Sunday mornings included worship in the sanctuary. The privilege to continue to worship the Triune God, Father, Son, and Holy Spirit was still ours to claim and to enjoy, but the influence of the Nazi philosophy was evident on the secular educational level.

When I reached Kindergarten age, I was sent to public school. There our Nazi teachers taught us a verse, which we said before meals. It went like this: *"Roll o roll, mein Topf ist voll, mein Bauch ist leer, mir hungerts sehr."* Translated it goes like this: "Roll o roll, my kettle is full, my stomach is empty, I am very hungry." After the meal the verse went like this: *"Roll o roll, mein Bauch ist voll, mein Topf ist leer, mir hungerts nicht mehr."* The translation is this: "Roll o roll, my stomach is full, my kettle is empty, I am no longer hungry." As one can note, absent is any notion of thanksgiving to God, any concept of gratitude for Him who is the giver of all things. I recognize this now as an effort of the Nazis to replace God centered mealtime prayers with humanistic nonsense.

*   *   *

The Nazi influence was not only there in the Kindergarten School. I witnessed it on the street where we lived. One day I was in the back of our house, the street side, when I noticed "marching" women passing by. These women wore light gray blankets, with a hole in the middle for their head and neck. They were carrying spades. Along side of them were German soldiers with their guns, all marching into Rheinsberg. Once more I did not understand this strange development that was happening right before me. Again I ran into the house to inquire from my mother what this meant. Graciously she declared that these were wealthy, noble, Jewish women, who were being forced by Hitler to do the hard labor of digging a deep ditch in Rheinsberg to slow the Russian movement into Germany. Of course, I was told later, that a hand grenade or a tank shot could easily fill in parts of the ditch to allow the war machinery to move forward unhindered.

On the way back from their hard labor, in the late afternoon, again I noticed these women marching by, but they halted at my grandfather's pond for washing up. The pond was located almost across from our farmstead. Once the women had finished washing themselves, they came close to our place and began picking up some of the apples and pears that had fallen down between the street and our fence. Soon those were gone, and I began to throw more over the fence to them. Immediately I noticed the German soldiers again, but this time they were not marching but brutally whipping the women, using the butt of their guns. All the while, they were swearing, cursing, and demanding the women stay away from this "super race" German boy. I wept.

MY FAMILY'S CIVIL DISOBEDIENCE

For Mother and for all other farmers economic life was tough. The Nazi government had determined quotas for how many commodities - grain, hogs, milk, and eggs - each farmer would have to deliver without remuneration. All of this was for the benefit of the soldiers and the *Vaterland*, fatherland. To achieve this requirement Mother was forced to deliver almost all of the grain, hogs, milk, and eggs produced on her little farm. Life was difficult and stressful for Mother. She was not used to managing a farm and missed Father's skills. Meeting her required quotas was just about impossible, but she trusted in the Lord to provide.

Adding to her stress from the economic demands made by the Nazis, a Nazi representative presented a large Nazi flag to Mother and ordered her to fly it in the center of our farm. The flag consisted of a field of red, a white circle, and inside it a swastika in black. Since clothing for civilians was very hard to get, Mother saw something else when she looked at that flag, namely, dress material for herself and for Elmire. Using fabric she had on hand and the flag, she cut dress configurations and soon had one for Elmire and one for herself. These dresses were beautiful. The Nazi representative, when he learned of this defilement of the Nazi flag, was livid. Again it was Mother's three sons who saved her from any retribution. Hitler did love his potential soldiers.

One December day in 1944, while I was visiting my grandfather, he and I did something that was illegal under the Nazi law. We secretly took his huge cell-powered radio down into the basement and tuned from the law approved German station to the unapproved BBC to hear what was happening in the war. Upstairs we listened to *Rundfunk Deutschland*, Radio Germany, where the news was always good - Germany was winning the war, acquiring more land, capturing many enemy soldiers – but in the basement we listened to the BBC. Grandfather was convinced that the British provided much more accurate information than the German radio station. From the BBC we probably heard some propaganda too, but we also heard the needed facts of the war, especially the progress being made by the Russian front, which was rapidly moving into Poland. Grandfather quietly met with other family members and other Christians and emphasized that the decisions about dealing with this grave situation needed to be made soon even though Christmas was near.

*   *   *

Christmas of 1944 came. Santa was good to my siblings and me. He asked that we sing some Christmas carols for him and recite some poems focused on Christmas. I do not recall what my siblings received, but I do recall that I got a real Santa Claus airplane. In order to see it best, I hung it from our kitchen light fixture, the most prominent place I could think of. Santa and the economy were not so good for my mother on her little farm as he was for us children. We each received a toy and an apple. How few were the gifts we received compared to what children receive today; yet we were happy and grateful.

The joy of the season was not the only thing on the minds and hearts of the adults. Christ's birth was a source of much joy, true, but the political scene was a source of much consternation. According to the BBC, Russia was moving westward rapidly, and our area would soon fall into the hands of the Russians. Reports surfaced on how the Germans who had remained in Bessarabia and accepted Communist rule had been treated. The information said that adult males had been sent to the Ural Mountains, there to dig for salt or coal. A very high percentage of them froze to death, starved to death, or were executed. Many women had been placed on a *Kolkhoz*, a huge collective farm, doing hard labor. Other more attractive women had been used as sexual partners for the Communist leaders. The children had been placed in collective schools, where they were indoctrinated in the Communist philosophy. This information weighed heavily on the adults, especially in light of the BBC news, and gave more than enough reasons to avoid the Communists again. But in addition to those grave thoughts, these former Bessarabian Germans could not help but wonder if those who had stayed in Bessarabia had been treated so horribly, how the Russians would treat those who had rejected their teachings and left. Plans had to be made immediately as how best to avoid the advancing Communist Russians. The BBC was monitored, and the planning commenced and continued in earnest.

The need for plans was confirmed for us by the arrival of some of the 200 to 280 thousand refugees who fled Latvia as the Russians approached.(http://www.rootssaknes.lv/Ethnicities/Latvians/Latvians_WWII.htm) These Latvians must have arrived in our village in the very early part of January 1945. I know that the weather was cold enough that our little pond was well frozen over. Our family befriended one of the Latvian families. Among their children was a boy about my age. He and I made immediate plans to skate on the frozen pond. The problem was we had no ice skates. After much thought we decided to use the wooden shoes we sometimes wore and modify them with some stiff wire. We got the shoes out, cut the wire nearly the length of the shoes, bent the ends of the wires with great effort, sharpened the ends, and "nailed" those wire ends into the soles of the wooden shoes. We had skates, not the best, but they afforded us much of the joy we had anticipated. The Latvians did not remain long in Rheinsberg. I do not remember exactly when they left, but by the time we were ready to go, they had already gone. They probably left a week or so before we did.

PLANS FOR LEAVING

It seemed obvious that we must go west to escape the advancing Russian army. The hope was that we would go west far enough to find the British, French, or American troops. We had heard that these soldiers were decent, moral, and kind. That was truly good news. We did not expect perfection because there is only one who is without sin, and He was hung on a cross. The difficult challenge confronting us was how to find these "enemy" soldiers.

Mass transportation was no longer available. All trains, busses, and even ships on the Baltic were already overloaded or so destroyed by bombings that travel in that way was out of the question. That meant we were on our own. Since winter had already set in and we were a family with small children – Adolf had just had his fourth birthday December 30th - travel by bicycle or on foot would be difficult, if not impossible. The consensus of opinion was that the best choice for the group was to use farm wagons, drawn by horses. We had a suitable wagon and a good team in Lise and Fuchs, who had replaced the aging Lotte. It was a much better plan than having us children walk what could be, a long, long, way.

That decision was easy, but there were other questions to be answered. How much more would fit in and around us children in the wagon? We would need fodder for the horses, food for the family, and a certain number of personal belongings. Would there be room enough for everything? Would we be able to come back later to get some of what we had left behind? Who would lead this whole group of folks? Who would decide the best route to get our grandparents, our aunts, our friends, and us safely to the west? Despite many prayers, there seemed to be no easy and fast answers to these and other questions.

Among the group most of the discussion centered on how long we would need to be gone. Some thought it would be at the most two weeks, or even less. Others thought it would take a long time for the German army to force the Russians from Poland, if ever. The decisions concerning what and how much to take centered on this question. But no one could be entirely sure how long or how short the time would be. Prayer gave comfort, which was good, because again we would need to rely daily on God's sufficient grace to lead and provide, just as we had done when we left Bessarabia, Austria, and even Topolno.

THE TREK BEGINS

By January 21, 1945, plans and preparatory details for fleeing to the west were complete. Unlike the hooped and canvas-covered Conestoga wagons which traveled across the plains of the United States, our dear Stachek had modified our best wagon with an A-framed superstructure, covered with boards and then with tar, throw rugs, more tar, blankets and still more tar. This provided insulation and protection from the cold and wet we were likely to encounter. Mother and Agnes had butchered and roasted a pig and several chickens and placed them into milk cans that were hung on the outside of the wagon between the wheels, trusting that our dear Lord God would provide the freezing temperature to keep the meat from spoiling. In the wagon we placed sacks of oats and other fodder for the horses, food items for us, and feather beds to keep us warm. Two moveable blankets were hung at the front allowing us to peek out, but keeping the strong cruel winds from blowing into the wagon.

Stachek had fully boarded the back of the wagon, which added additional protection from severe weather.

Mother also brought photos, legal papers, the two Bibles that had been brought from Bessarabia containing the genealogical family trees of my mother and father. She also brought the hand-loomed blanket made by her great-grandmother, which had been her parents' wedding present. We took no clothing except what we had on our bodies upon leaving. These few material possessions were the only things she took with us; all else was left behind.

I'm sure there were many precious personal belongings she regretted having to leave behind, such as some newly acquired furniture, changes of clothing, and remembrances of my father. At that time, however, I was not thinking of things like that. While seated in the covered wagon as we were departing, I was still begging Mother to let me take along my Santa Claus airplane. I could see it through the window, hanging underneath the kitchen light fixture. She lovingly responded with this saddening fact, "Horst, if you take your airplane, then Elmire can take her doll, Adolf his toy, and Fritz his, and we just do not have the space for them. I am so sorry." I felt very sad. I could not even take my one Christmas present with me. Now my loss seems so small and insignificant when I compare it with what my parents and grandparents left behind in Bessarabia and each stop along the way.

Again, as Father did in Bessarabia, we set all the animals free so they could forage on their own. We released our newly acquired young German shepherd from his chain, hoping he would run along with us as we fled.

It was cold and clear on January 21st as our wagon joined the other wagons in the middle of Rheinsberg. Our grandparents' wagon, holding my mother's parents and her sisters - Klara, Elfriede, and Nelly - lined up just ahead of ours. I do not remember exactly how many wagons left that day, but it seemed to be at least a dozen. The talk of the town was that we would be returning within a few weeks.

Perhaps the wishful thinking of our return was a blessing in disguise for Mother because knowledge of the courage it would take to face the many challenges that lay ahead would have been daunting. I was not leaving with my Santa Claus airplane, but our young German shepherd was running along beside us. Knowing this gave my siblings and me "something" to take along that was, in a way, just ours. It was a small bit of reassurance for us.

Since we lived on the east side of the Wisla River and our trek was to the west, we headed out of Rheinsberg to the river. Much, much to our surprise, the bridge we had crossed so many times before was no longer there! I'm sure this caused much consternation because the Wisla is quite a large river. I do not know the actual width of the river at this point, but my guess is that it was about a half-kilometer wide (approximately 550 yards) and also fairly deep. The Germans had dismantled the bridge, knowing it would slow down the rapidly approaching Russian army and give Germany a little more breathing room. The road, as it approached and met the river, was much higher than the water level. The task of getting all the wagons down the steep embankment was a horrific task. The farm wagons were not equipped with any sort of brakes, but somehow the horses, with the help of the men, managed to get them to the river, thank God.

Once we were at the water's level, the distinct fear was what would happen when our three-inch wide, steel rimed wagon wheels rolled onto the ice. Would the ice break? And if the ice held, would it continue to hold the weight of all the wagons as they crossed the river?

While we were waiting for our turn, I was amazed by the frozen vastness, both up and down river. Ahead of us, men seemed to be pounding the ice with steel poles. They then left some markers and proceeded to pound and mark all the way across the Wisla. When our turn to cross came, Mother held the halter of one horse, and Aunt Nelly, Mother's youngest sister, held the halter of the other horse. My older brother Fritz, who was twelve, was on the wagon in the driver's seat, holding the reins. Getting the horses to walk on the ice was a fearful challenge. We slowly proceeded across the river, following the men with their poles, aided by the sufficient grace of God and surely some angelic help. It wasn't until much later, in 2004, that I understood what the men with the poles were doing. A man from Canada, who was also wintering in Arizona, as we were, explained to me that a "sounding" can be heard and the particular sound heard registers the depth and quality of the ice. He had done a lot of ice fishing where similar tools are used to establish the depth and quality of the ice and assured me that cars and pickups can be driven on the ice safely.

The missing bridge had crossed the river at one of the narrower places. Our leaders decided to make the crossing there, thinking it would allow us to get us off the ice more quickly. Many, many prayers were said, aloud and silently, and God allowed us safe passage. We did not know that where a river is narrow, the water underneath runs faster and deeper, compared to a wide riverbed, which allows the same quantity of waters to flow much more shallowly and slowly. Reports came to us sometime later that some wagons in another group broke through the ice, ending in tragedy. Thinking about their demise and what could have happened to us sends shivers deep down into my soul.

The embankment on the other side of the river again challenged the teams to pull the wagons up the very steep slope. By God's grace and with the assistance of many people, this burdensome job was also completed successfully. As the men and horses labored to get the wagons up the incline, we could hear the piercing tank units of the Russian army pounding loudly on the east side of the Wisla.

The weather was often very cold. I understand that the winter of '45 was one of the coldest and snowiest in the area across northern Poland, where we were fleeing. Our horses often had icicles hanging from their mouths and often had to pull the wagon through snow that was up to their bellies. Many times the lead wagon stopped for some unknown reason, causing the wagons in the rear to ram the wagon ahead of them because they were not able to stop in time. Our dear Stachek, who continued to travel with us as far as the Oder River, was always ready with hammer and nails to repair our wagon, which Mother deeply appreciated. What a good thing the back of the wagon had been boarded up, or the tongue of the following offending wagon would have found its way into the wagon where we were riding and caused injury.

Many of the Germans who had been resettled into Poland as we had been adopted the Nazi's philosophy and treated the Poles as if they were slaves. These Germans looked upon themselves as a super race. The mistreated Polish citizens resented and hated them, and often these abused Poles retaliated by stealing, cheating, and even physically abusing their abusers. Since Mother did not treat Stachek and Agnes as the Nazis demanded, our Polish helpers remained most helpful, courteous, and kind to Mother and us children. Our prayers went with Stachek when he had to stay in Poland when we reached the Oder River, the border between Poland and Germany. We often wondered what became of Stachek and Agnes during and after the war.

To my knowledge, my paternal grandparents left Alt-Posttal when we did. They were relocated into Poland with their adult daughters. In 1945 they fled to Heilbronn, Germany, to avoid the Russians. Later, they moved to Markgröningen, Germany, living in a town house with their daughter and son-in-law, Frieda and John Gäckle, and their single daughters Lydia and Olga.

PROBLEMS ALONG THE WAY

The extreme cold contributed to a problem, which I do not remember but was told about later. My health seemed to deteriorate rapidly. My body temperature fell, and I was unable to take nourishment. I reached the point where I was unresponsive. No doctors were traveling on our trek or other treks near ours. It would have been quite unusual if they had been. Most medical personnel were busy with the injured and maimed soldiers on the fronts and were rarely available to civilians. How the prayers must have flown to heaven on my behalf. My Aunt Klara, having been trained in first aid by the Red Cross, became God's messenger of mercy for me. She came on our wagon and began to stimulate my circulatory system by vigorously rubbing me. She wrapped me in blankets and held me close to herself inside her coat. Eventually she was able to get me to take some liquids and nourishment. Her efforts were blessed with His sufficiency, and I responded favorably. Did I have an infection, dehydration, hypothermia, or something else? I don't know. I only know that it was through God's grace and Aunt Klara that I recovered.

It was some days later when the wagons stopped in a village, and we all were welcomed into a warm home and treated to a hot, nourishing meal, a bath, and a warm place to sleep. For weeks we had been confined to the wagon, traveling even during the night to stay ahead of the approaching Russian army. We had been living on the frozen meats from the milk cans Mother had tied to the side of the wagon. Mother thawed pieces of the previously cooked chicken or pork by holding them under her arm to thaw them enough that we could manage to eat them. Our drinking water was melted snow. We did little, if any, washing of either bodies or clothing because we did not stop except for brief periods to rest the horses. Even if there had been a ready source of water, we did not have a way to dry anything that would have been washed. We even got used to the lack of privacy and having to use the makeshift toilet as the wagon rolled on. This village "oasis" was a benefit for our horses too, since they were warmed inside a shed and given some nourishing fodder. I wonder if the Latvians who stopped at our farm appreciated our hospitality as much as we appreciated the kindness and generosity of this wonderful village. The relentless efforts of the Russian army with their penetrating tank units, however, could be heard as we awoke, and we again moved westward, thankful for those who had so warmly welcomed us and nourished our bodies and souls. On the entire trek I remember stopping like this only twice.

The fodder we had brought along was soon exhausted; the generous provision of fodder from the villages we had passed through was no longer available. The folks from here on west had given all they could to earlier travelers and, of course, to Hitler's required allotments to the *Vaterland.* They did not allow us access to their barns or sheds, as the folks to the east had. The horses were getting so thin one could easily count their ribs, and Mother had to do what she never thought she would have to do. She, along with a few other adults, did what the gypsies have done, or so I am told. These adults divided up into two groups. One group went to the front of a farmhouse, getting the attention of the owners. They asked for a chance to meet as many of their family as possible and enjoyed a heart-warming chat. In the meantime, the other group found their way, now free of detection, into the barn where some hay and oats were still stored in hiding. They began to help themselves to it, knowing that the owners were duly preoccupied.

Mother was in this latter group. She wore a huge apron and so was chosen to carry the hay, while the others of this second group helped themselves to the oats. Just at this moment, the air raid siren announced a major air raid, and, sure enough, the planes came. They began their air attack with bullets flying, some of them hitting the gable of this now *bestolen*, robbed, home. Bricks fell in all directions, and a clump landed just inches in front of Mother, knocking the hay out of her apron. Had she been a few inches forward, her life would have come to a certain end.

Her comments about this incident later were, "Had I been killed by that clump of falling bricks, what would my dear heavenly Father have said to me, breaking one of his commandments, the one 'You shall not steal.' Would He have forgiven me?" Would God have understood her reasons - that stealing fodder to feed those starving horses could ultimately save her life and her children's lives? Would the Lord have forgiven her lack of trust in Him? "These questions will be answered on the 'other side,'" my mother observed. She proceeded back to the horses without any hay that day. Somehow the horses did not die of starvation, and she never again chose to break God's Commandments but trusted that He would provide for her, her children, and for her team - Lise and Fuchs.

Mother spoke of this team, saying they gave their best. Even at that, the horses were ready to quit. They fell, due to weakness or, at times, due to the road surface, but each time, she and other people would rub the horses down, give them some fodder (I do not know from where, since ours was long exhausted) and some short periods of standing still – a brief rest from pulling their ever heavy load. And when the word was given to move on, by the grace of God, we did, always being goaded by the advancing Russian tank units.

When she recalled this journey, Mother would share, with deep feelings, the heartache of parents who were traveling with tiny babies. How difficult it was to provide proper care for them. Some wee little ones made it; others did not. The deceased one's burial was most brief, and the burial place was somewhere along the road, covered with snow, as there was no time to dig into the ground, and the ground was all too frozen anyway.

*   *   *

For some time we had been looking forward to reaching the *Autobahn,* Germany's super highway. We knew it would bring our tired horses a respite from the deep snow and frozen ruts of the back roads we had been traveling for so long. Finally we reached our goal, but with the *Autobahn* came something we had not anticipated – lots of traffic. There were civilians fleeing the war – some on foot carrying their meager possessions, those making slightly better time on bicycles, and many like us in wagons. There were also members of the retreating German army. Some of these war-torn, bedraggled German soldiers were on foot, but quite a few had the luxury of riding in dilapidated army vehicles. All of us were heading west.

One evening as the ever more lengthening and darkening shadows surrounded the countryside, the world around us was pierced again with another blast of siren sounds, announcing a coming air raid. Mother was told by some of the retreating soldiers to hold onto the horses' halters to keep them from bolting and running should the ensuing sounds spook them. If the bombs should fall nearby, they continued, she should immediately fall to the pavement to avoid shrapnel or flying debris, which might injure or kill her. Then, they felt, she would be much safer in a prone position. In the meantime, Aunt Klara had come to our wagon and had us children follow her. She led us off our wagon, away from the pavement, through the ditch, and into a pine tree forest, although I remember the trees did not seem as tall and protecting as some pines usually are.

Soon the sounds of the coming airplanes could be heard. From the heavens strips of aluminum came falling down. They were about a foot and a half long and about two inches wide. I enjoyed the task of catching them before my siblings could. Later I learned from a US bombardier who had served in World War II that these strips were dropped by the Allied airplanes to confuse the radar of the defensive artillery of the German units on the ground.

Very soon, we heard strange sounds. Aunt Klara told us these sounds were bombs falling in our direction. Before long we could hear a change in sound, which indicated that a bomb was coming and it was likely to hit near or on us. With fear and trepidation Aunt Klara held us close to her, anticipating the bomb's impact. Maybe ten to fifteen yards from us the bomb fell. It did not explode, but it did make a large hole, perhaps seven or eight yards deep and about twelve to fifteen yards across at the top. Dirt flew, even as our feelings flew from sheer fear to grateful thanksgiving once we realized we were all still alive.

At about the same time Mother, who had stayed with the horses to keep them from spooking, tearing their harness, and running, obediently fell to the pavement each time a bomb fell in the area. She did just as she had been directed to do by the retreating soldiers. Remarkably, none of the bombs that fell on the pavement or in the ditch in our immediate vicinity exploded. I have been told that a portion of the many bombs assembled are duds and that for one mechanical reason or another they will not explode on impact, even on solid surfaces. However, the percentage of duds is extremely low. That evening and night far more bombs fell unexploded than the normal percentage of duds could explain. These non-exploding bombs soon gave Mother a sense of confidence and peace, and she no longer fell to the ground, even though more bombs fell close to her. We concluded these bombs did not explode because of the sufficient grace of our loving, caring, protecting God. We experienced firsthand that when we are in the midst of events we would never choose, we see even more clearly God's sufficient grace. How sad it is for those who do not believe in a higher power, in a beneficent being, in an all knowing and all powerful God, who commands a host of angels. We wish that everyone could join us in our faith walk and know the peace and comfort that comes from the knowledge of His love and divine care.

After a long, long night the dawn revealed the reason for the Allied air attack in this particular area. Our fleeing had brought us to the place where the *Autobahn* crossed a dual railroad track system connecting Berlin and Stettin by huge overpasses. Destroying the overpasses would stop the traffic on both the rails and on the *Autobahn*. This was wise strategy on the part of the Allies, but by God's intervening grace their goal was not met, and we could continue fleeing safely westward.

The goal for the Allies to destroy both modes of traffic had noble intentions. Berlin is the German capitol from which many a dictate would be sent to Stettin, where a major war machinery support system had been established. Once the traffic on the rail system was stopped, the German support for its war efforts would be drastically reduced. Probably the *Autobahn,* too, was important for the German war support system, and destroying its bridges would reduce suffering and death by bringing the war to an end more quickly.

THE TREK ENDS IN GYHUM

Not until April 9, 1945, did our trek reach its end. We had been fleeing for eighty days and nights, having left Rheinsberg on January 21st. Our stopping point was between Hamburg and Bremen in a small village by the name of Gyhum, which was located between the Elbe River to the east and the Weser River to the west, both flowing into the North Sea. Apparently mayors from cities and villages in this part of Germany had anticipated the many *Flüchtlinge*, fleeing people, because when we arrived, it was known which communities could receive refugees, even which families could house additional occupants. Often more than one family was placed into a single house.

The officials also knew what we would be bringing with us. We had lice! These creatures had settled into our bedding, onto our skin and hair, and acted as if they would be our lifelong friends. Members of the community who did not have lice and did not want them worked to rid us of our companions. We were met by men and women, who were holding big tubes with handles sticking out of one end. Moving the handle in and out of the tube produced a white dust that was puffed onto our clothing, between our clothing and body, in our hair, and on our bedding and possessions - seemingly everywhere. Goodbye, parasites!

We were placed into a house owned by a family by the name of Ficken. Mrs. Ficken lived there with her two sons. Her husband was away fighting with the German army. Another fleeing couple by the name of Rosenow was placed there also. All three families lived in the house/barn unit that was typical of the homes in rural Germany. Our quarters consisted of two rooms. There was a kitchen, perhaps three yards wide and six yards deep, and a bedroom, about six yards by seven yards, where all five of us slept. Mother slept with Elmire, I slept with Adolf, and Fritz had his own bed. There was not much room to move around.

Our kitchen had previously been the room for the hired hand, so it contained no stove or sink such as is normally found in a kitchen. We did have a very small pot-bellied stove on which only one item could be heated at a time. The chimney was a metal pipe from the stove, which went up some distance and then out the window. One pane of the window had been removed, and sheet metal with a hole for the pipe was put in to replace the pane. Here we did our cooking, one item at a time. It took coordination on Mother's part to get everything for a meal done and hot at the same time. At times the effort of starting the fire was ruefully hindered by the outside winds blowing the smoke right back into our kitchen. Mother had watering eyes, and all of us did a lot of coughing. In addition to the stove, there was a table, a bench, and, I believe, a chair or two, as well as a small hutch for our few utensils and grocery items. The bedroom had a *Schrank*, a moveable clothes closet, as well as the beds, and in the wall of the bedroom was a *Kachelofen*, a glazed tile-heating oven, fired with peat, wood, or coal, to keep us warm.

We had no indoor plumbing. Our water had to be carried from a hand pump located in another part of the house. The water came from a *Brunnen,* a well, which did not have the cleanest water, but we drank it and lived. The outhouse was next to the hog house, where the odor of both the hogs and humans often grossly offended our olfactory systems.

The dear Rosenows had only one room, about the size of our bedroom, requiring them to use blankets to divide their room into several sections. True, there were only the two of them, but their facility was very crowded. Safety and the respite from the seemingly never-ending trek made their spirits high despite the cramped living conditions.

Mrs. Rosenow, although she had no children of her own, had a good sense of humor and used it in dealing with us children in the close quarters when we were too noisy or too active in our play. In order to quiet us, she advised Mother to pound three nails into the kitchen wall and hang us three children on them in order to slow us down. The thought of seeing one of my siblings hanging on a nail by the collar made me laugh, but the thought of my hanging there quieted me down for a while. On another occasion when I had come in from the outside, quite wet from the rain, she advised me on how to stay dry even while I was outside in the rain. She told me to run very fast, thereby getting underneath and past the raindrops before they could fall and hit me. Well, I tried it. I was even more soaked than before. She remained firm. I should run even much faster than I did, only then would I remain dry. Again I failed, or her advice failed. When I came in, totally soaked from head to toe, she laughed and said that she must have been wrong. Truly, I was "all wet" in this case. She did a great job of tiring me out with her humorous approach. It was better psychology than complaining of my boisterousness.

Once we arrived in Gyhum we had no particular use for our two horses, Lisa and Fuchs, or for our wagon. Mother decided to sell them all to the farm owner, hoping to get enough to purchase shoes and clothing for each of us, as well as a little to set aside. The money being used at that time (spring/summer of 1945) was the *Reichsmark*. She had the two horses and the wagon appraised and received what seemed the appropriate amount of money. Little did she or anyone else know that the financial restructuring of the German economy, the *Wehrung*, was planned. The *Reichsmark* was replaced by the *Deutsche Mark*. This meant that all the money Mother had received for her items would have to be traded in for the new money. The restructuring resulted in a major devaluation. For the handfuls of *Reichsmarks* from the sale, she could get but a few *Deutsche Marks*. She could purchase only one pair of shoes, and one item of clothing with this new money, not anything else. Again she was at the very short end of the stick.

She had lost usage of the money used in Bessarabia, the Romanian *Leu*; it was nearly valueless against the *Reichsmark* anyway. Now she lost the usage of the *Reichsmark*, and it was nearly valueless against the *Deutsche Mark*. And true to pattern, her *D Mark* was worth less than a fourth of a dollar when she ultimately exchanged it in America. After a few years in the USA Mother received from the German government what was called *Lasten Ausgleich*, an equalization of burden payment. Her losses in Bessarabia were given a certain value and a minute portion of that value was then sent to her while she was living in Alden, Minnesota. Of course, since the German *Deutsche Mark* was valued at only a fourth of the US dollar, her payment from Germany was quite small.

The Ficken/Hastedt house in Gyhum, where the Hehr family was allowed two rooms - a kitchen area, and one bedroom. The two windows below the veranda provided a view of the neighbor's house across the street when it was bombed and burned.

Horst, Elmire, and Adolf in much needed, though mismatched, clothing provided by Lutheran World Relief.

Grandfather Eduard Tetzlaff, Mrs. Rosenau, and Theodore, a family friend.

THE WESTERN FRONT ARRIVES

Hardly had we become acquainted with the premises and the Ficken family, Mimmie and her two sons, Werner and Helmut, than we were told that the Western Front would be at Gyhum soon and we were to get ready. This meant taking our bedding into the basement and stockpiling candles, food, and water supplies there. In order to avoid shrapnel entering the part of the basement where we were to stay, we filled sacks with sand and placed them over all of the basement windows except the one that was sheltered by a veranda constructed of concrete. This would give us some daylight should the electricity be interrupted by the entering Western Front bombings. All three families crowded into one end of the basement. Being together in such close quarters for days while the war continued just outside the window proved to be quite stressful.

Since the season was spring, all of Mimmie's 25 or so cows were driven out of Gyhum to the pastures about five kilometers, three miles, away. It was felt that the cows would probably be safer there than in a building should it be bombed. I do not remember what they did with their six horses, the two dozen, or so, hogs, and their chickens in the approaching moments of the actual confrontation of the Allied and the Axis powers.

What I do remember is the arrival of two German SS soldiers. They came down into the basement where we were cowering and trying to hide. They saluted with their indoctrinated *"Heil Hitler,"* right arms stretched out, somewhat raised. We responded with a scary *"Guten Tag,"* Good Day. My mother told them they should give up and admit defeat because the war was almost over. They arrogantly retorted with words to the effect that they would never yield to those "cardboard" soldiers of the Allied forces. They looked around and left by the one exit that led out of the basement directly into the orchard. We heard some shots, and later their dead bodies were found under the fruit trees. How tragic their lives had to end because they believed the indoctrination promulgated by Hitler.

*   *   *

Almost on the heels of the exiting German soldiers, a solitary Allied soldier entered. As we had been instructed, we raised our arms in surrender to reduce any potential conflict. With time our arms grew tired and we lowered them. The soldier appeared to be very young, was thin and short, and perspired profusely. He held a machine gun in one hand and had hand grenades and bullets hung on his body. He spoke a language we did not understand. Finally he said over and over, "Nazis, Nazis?" With his other hand and his body bent, he directed his flashlight all around the basement room, even under our beds.

Finally he seemed satisfied with his search, posed a faint smile, set his machine gun next to our bed, took off his heavy helmet revealing his very sweaty hair, and wiped his perspiring forehead. He spoke again, but we could not follow his words. Having spotted a line of bottles sitting on a ledge of simple boards to his left, he pointed to them, said more, pointed to his mouth and pretended to be drinking.

Mimmie, having placed there the bottles filled with juices made from raspberries and other harvests from her extensive garden during the preceding summer, got his gist and gave him one. He smiled more obviously, opened the bottle, tasted it, drank the contents, and with a motion over his stomach signaled delight and that he was refreshed. We were all relieved that he was apparently satisfied with the drink.

To show his gratitude, he reached into one of his many pockets and held an item in the direction of us children. His smile seemed directed to us children, and he said the word *gift*, repeating it several times. Our response was not what he expected. In the German language the word *Gift* means poison. My, what confusion! What renewed fear! We were sure he was coming to us children with a smile to trick us and poison us. Mother and Mimmie were stunned. Would their children go forward and take this *Gift* from the smiling soldier? Well, one did go. I was the foolish one. I got closer to him, looked at his offering, and wondered if it could be a wrapping of candy or even a chocolate bar. Mother's thoughts were filled with trepidation, wondering what her foolish son was doing. The offered, questionable item, now in my hand, looked like a bar. I opened it most cautiously and held it close to my nose to smell it. It smelled like chocolate. Yes, it appeared to be a chocolate bar and not poison. I broke off a piece and slowly tasted it. Yes, yes, it was chocolate, something none of us had had for months! The other children got some too, but I got the biggest piece. What a treat it was!

It appeared that our hopes and prayers had been answered in the guise of this smiling, friendly, kind, and moral young British soldier. We recognized immediately his courtesy and respect shown to Mother, Mimmie, and Mrs. Rosenow, lovely, pretty women. Moreover, we realized that the reason for our trek, to avoid the Communist Russians for good, had been accomplished. May God be forever glorified, for we believe this was accomplished by the gift of His sufficient grace.

The arrival of the Allies and the Western Front meant more bombing raids. The house/barn combination located just across the street from the house where we were living was bombed. Several airplanes dropped their incendiary bombs on the L-shaped structure, and in no time the whole building was aflame. We watched the fire rage firsthand from our one uncovered basement window, through the veranda. Before long, we could smell the results of the firestorm raging there. Apparently all the cows and horses still in the barn were ablaze. Fortunately, by God's grace the owners of that burning house/barn combination and the displaced persons living with them were able to escape and survived the tragedy. Burning flesh has a unique odor. Having once smelled it, one will never forget. A Salvation Army officer and friend from Clinton, who had been sent to New York City shortly after the 9-11 tragedy, confirmed this. He told us that the two things that were most impressed on him were the size of the rubble and the smell of the still rising smoke of burning flesh.

There was other damage near us. The house/barn located across the other street from ours was also bombed, but only the barn part was destroyed, and the family escaped unharmed. Next door to us, adjacent to the *Brunnen* and baking oven, lived Pastor Jasper and his lovely family. The parsonage in which they lived, the adjacent confirmation instruction hall, and the only church (Lutheran) in Gyhum escaped the attack unscathed. God and His angels must have been very busy.

Many buildings were bombed and leveled to the ground in Gyhum, including the one where my grandparents were quartered. They were living in the house of the *Burgermeister*, the mayor of Gyhum, *Herr*, Mr. Fahjen. They described all aspects of the bombing in detail, but all that I remember is their telling of the tremendous noise of the bricks and beams collapsing upon their shelter in the basement, and, even more surprising, the huge quantities of dust gushing into their midst. No preparations had been made to deal with the dust. Quickly, they made makeshift protective masks by wetting towels to place over their mouth and nose to keep them from breathing in so much of the horrible dust. Despite the bombing there, no person was hurt or killed. How Mother thanked God that her parents and three sisters were still alive!

The dance hall in Gyhum was untouched by the bombing, and it became the new home for my maternal grandparents. They moved to a good-sized apartment on the second floor above a large dance floor and stage on the first floor. Many plays, such as "Little Red Riding Hood" and "Hansel and Gretel" were presented on the stage. Dances were held almost every Saturday evening. Grandfather and Grandmother differed on the concept of dancing. Grandfather encouraged dancing, done with due respect and without ulterior motives. Grandmother thought dancing should be prohibited altogether. Their children and grandchildren chose between Grandfather's advice and Grandmother's advice. Grandfather became my adult male role model and my counselor. I spent much of my free time with him and looked forward to when I could be with him again and again. Hence it is no surprise that I chose Grandfather's advice and so learned how to waltz, polka, foxtrot and do the two-step.

$$* \qquad * \qquad *$$

"Our" home remained intact. Not that efforts to destroy it were not made; they just failed. Once the Western Front had passed, I remember that men came to the house and literally picked up several unexploded bombs. A few had fallen on the side where the huge oven used for baking bread stood not far from the *Brunnen.* A few bombs were also found lying unexploded on the other side of our house where the big orchard was located. We were warned not to touch these bombs because of their latent ability to explode. We were to leave that to qualified people who would remove them and take them somewhere safer. Years later many incendiary devices were still being found, sometimes when they were accidentally triggered by an animal, person, or farm implement.

THE BRITISH OCCUPATION

Not long after the front passed, on May 8, 1945, the war finally ended. The small village of Gyhum, which was comprised of the homesteads of the farmers in the area, was overrun with the British occupation forces. There were always soldiers around, and near each house were parked two or three British tanks. Some were so closely parked that one could hardly walk between the tanks and the buildings. The occupation lasted for the next several months.

These were tough times for my younger brother, Adolf, especially when an airplane flew over. The sound of a plane caused him to flee what he imagined would be imminent bombing raids. He would leave the room as quickly as he could. If he were in the kitchen, he would run to the window and jump out although it was four or five feet to the ground below. If he were in our bedroom, he would run to the basement, again for the protection he thought he needed. Despite the repeated loving, patient reassurances that the war was over and there would be no more bombing, Adolf's emotional memory would not let him relax. It took a long time for him to "forget" the bombings associated with airplanes. Today he would be treated for post-traumatic stress disorder.

Another concern during the occupation centered on the attention one of the soldiers gave my five-year-old sister. Elmire was a beautiful little girl with dark eyes and wavy black hair. The soldier would come from his Jeep parked some yards from the house/barn, pick her up in his arms, and take her to his canvas spread out on the grass, near his Jeep. This was very scary for Mother and probably for my sister too, wondering if he would hurt her, abuse her, or even steal her. It was my job to keep watch and report to Mother, just as Miriam had kept watch over her baby brother Moses when he was hidden in the rushes of the Nile.

Fortunately, I could report to Mother a most tender scene. The soldier gave Elmire candy, stroked her pretty face and hair, and said things in the language we did not understand with what seemed tears in his eyes at times. After a half hour or so he would bring her back, having both of her hands full of candy, which the rest of us siblings would willingly help her enjoy.

Mother, her sisters, and parents concluded that this British soldier must be the father of a girl much like Elmire, whom he missed so much that he assuaged some of his loneliness by sharing his parental love with our little German girl. I have to think that Elmire benefited from this fatherly kind of love also since her own father had died not that many years earlier. I find it ironic that as an adult my sister dated a young man from England for a while though she did not marry him.

*　　　*　　　*

Soon after the front passed by Gyhum, *Herr* Kubart, the local *Artz*, doctor, diagnosed me with severe malnutrition. His prescription was that I should eat at Mimmie's table, where more nourishing food was available. From then on, after school dismissed for the day, I went to their kitchen, where their hired help, Mrs. Reichenberg, dished up some of the food she had kept back for me. My, how great that tasted, and I could eat until I felt I was satisfied. My strength began to build so that after a year or so at their table the food Mother was able to provide was almost adequate. Many a meal at Mother's table included a slice of very dark rye bread with lard and sugar spread on it and skim milk to drink. We often had soup for the evening meal, rarely meat, but many vegetables, more than enough potatoes, and lots of fruit. Fritz ate with the other hired hands he worked with, but Elmire and Adolf received only what Mother could provide.

Groceries were extremely limited at the grocery stores, and many items were rationed. Each family was given ration stamps, which would have to be used to purchase a particular item, such as sugar. In addition, Mother had very little money to purchase these limited items, so our cupboards were usually quite empty. For festive occasions extended families would save their stamps and pool them to purchase what would be needed to make a meal appropriate for the holiday or other occasion, such as Christmas, a wedding, or confirmation.

Eventually, additional nourishment was made available to nearly all children of displaced persons through the generosity of the USA. Right after school instead of going to the farmers' tables we took empty containers down to the other school building to be filled. There, ladies had cooked a soup or a cereal to supplement our daily food intake. The generous portions were tasty and eagerly anticipated.

As much as we felt the food shortages, we were fortunate to live in a farming community and not in one of the big cities. I recall beggars, whom we called *Hamsters*, from the cities like Hamburg or Bremen desperately begging from us in the country. They had huge rucksacks on their backs filled with clothing or other non-food items ready to barter for food. Butter, meat, flour, fruit, and vegetables were among the direly needed items by these desperate folks. On one occasion the *Hamster* was a member of the Hamburg Symphony, who had no items for barter, but he had a mighty trumpet. He came to Mimmie, asked what her favorite music was, and then played it beautifully for her. I saw tears in her eyes. I had never heard a trumpet played like he played. The professional musician got some butter and some meat and a hearty *Dankeschön*, thank you, from Mimmie.

For many displaced families, the one person who seemed to bring much joy and high hopes was the postal carrier. He traveled on a bicycle that had two huge baskets attached to it, one in front of him and one behind him. He was welcomed with warm smiles and great anticipation because just perhaps he had a package for them from America. Many families received huge packages of food items. These included flour, coffee, sugar, dried milk, candy, chocolate, and eggs. Yes, eggs were packed within the flour container in the package and shipped across the Atlantic. We, too, received such a desired package, and not one egg was broken, not even cracked. We felt that we were so very blessed with a package from America. I cannot recall if it came from some distant relative or from the church, but I do remember how delighted Mother was and how she enjoyed these "heavenly gifts," especially the real coffee. Roasted rye was a pathetic substitute. These packages were few and far in between, but they did show us the love and care of people in that great land where milk and honey flowed, America. Through these packages we got clues of what life might be like somewhere other than in war-torn, decimated Germany.

At some point in this time frame Mimmie received the devastating news that her husband had been killed on the Russian front and was no longer listed as missing in action. Her feelings about this vacillated from grief to relief. She did not want him to be caught by the Russians and imprisoned there, and she did not want him dead. She wanted him to come home to her and their two sons, Werner and Helmut. Yet, she consoled herself knowing that he was not enduring incredible abuse and starvation, confined as a prisoner in Communist Russia. Mother gave much comfort to Mimmie, since Mother had been walking in similar shoes with no husband at her side either and having children to rear in a world full of horrendous turmoil. It was sometime later that Mimmie remarried. Her second husband was her former farm manager, Mr. Hastedt. He was a kind man, who provided us with opportunities to make ends meet in any way he could.

At the opposite extreme of the devastating news of Mr. Ficken's death was the excitement and joy when Mother's two brothers came back home from their prisoner of war camps. *Onkel* Ernest had been in a Russian prison, and *Onkel* Johann had been in a Western Allies prison. The fact that both of my uncles came home alive was most unusual because most other German families I knew had lost at least one relative in the war. During the war Grandmother had been at prayer more than any close or distant relative I have ever known. At times she was on her knees even outside her home praying for her sons and the sons and daughters of other families she knew who were serving. Yes, Grandmother was most thankful that God had heard her many prayers for them all, and especially that her two sons had returned home alive.

Uncle Johann had been severely injured, receiving major damage to his intestines and stomach from shrapnel. He said that he had seen this shrapnel coming, slicing off some treetops and branches. Then, most unexpectedly, it veered in his direction and sliced into his body, flattening him instantly. After many surgeries he managed to heal enough to be able to walk. Later, after he returned, he was even able to do manual work in Zeven, riding there on his NSU motorcycle.

Uncle Ernst got a job in Gyhum, as a *Stellmacher*, a wheelwright. There Uncle Ernst "helped" Santa Claus fashion a scooter, which Santa then brought me at Christmas. I had a major toy again. What fun it was for me, to dismantle it, check it all out, reassemble it, and then ride it. But the far greater joy for all our relatives was to see our uncles home from the war.

SCHOOL IN GYHUM

At that time school went year-round with short, usually three week, vacations interspersed throughout the year, and it was necessary to continue with our education once the war ended. Since the confirmation instruction hall was still standing undamaged after the bombing of Gyhum, it was chosen to house grades one through four. The old school building, also undamaged, housed grades five through eight. Teachers were assigned – *Herr* Fiedler for the lower grades of one through four and *Herr* Intemann for the upper grades, five through eight. To us *Herr* Intemann seemed very old. He had been retired but was called out of his retirement during the war due to the tremendous shortage of teachers. He retired again after two more years of teaching, and *Herr* Kunzendorf replaced him.

Having missed school for several months during the time we were fleeing, I was happy to go back to school. In Rheinsberg I had almost finished the second grade so I was placed into the third grade with *Herr* Fiedler as my teacher. We had at least forty students, grades one through four, in that classroom. What a daunting task that must have been for *Herr* Fiedler!

*   *   *

The large pupil/teacher ratio was made more difficult by the lack of materials. We had no paper and pencils, only slate boards and a very few chalk pieces. There were no textbooks or teacher's guides either. We learned by rote memorization. Reciting the multiplication tables, the German language grammar rules, and other topics kept us busy from eight in the morning till one in the afternoon. From what I remember, discipline was a minor issue. We went to school Mondays through Saturdays. After class was dismissed at one p.m., the pupils went home and ate their noon meal there. Then, time was spent at the kitchen table memorizing assignments given at school. We had no study time to do any homework at school.

The same confirmation hall that served for the lower grades' schoolroom was also where I was presented a lesson in more than the three *r*'s of reading, (w)riting and (a)rithmatic. Ethics was not a part of our teacher's lesson, but it became a reality to me in that classroom.

I happen to be seated close to a son of the wealthiest family in the school district of Gyhum. He was of royal genealogy; his parents owned thousands of acres, a huge dairy, and many other holdings. One day in class I observed this boy picking up a new pencil sharpener from the desk of a child much, much poorer than he was and, thinking that no one was looking, put it into his pouch where his own many pencils and erasers were kept. He never returned the pencil sharpener. I know, because I asked the other child if he still had his pencil sharpener, and he replied that he must have lost it. I knew it had not been lost, but stolen.

The question for me was an ethical one. Should I tell on the thief, or should I remain quiet? Should the wealthy be allowed to steal from the poor and get by without consequences? All too often when a poor person steals from the wealthy, the consequences are enormous.

65

Would the teacher believe me, or would he believe the lies the boy would tell if he were confronted? If I told, would the rich boy take it out on the boy he had stolen from and on me, too? I still am not sure if not telling was the right thing. I know what I would do now. Stealing is stealing, no matter how royal or how poor, and equal penalties should apply.

Eventually, more learning tools became available, learning progressed significantly, and I moved into the upper grade classroom where *Herr* Kunzendorf taught. In addition to the reading, writing and arithmetic curriculum, we now added geometry, geography, history, religion, yes, religion, and *Schönschreiben*, writing that is beautiful, very legible.

I recall two incidents from my time in the upper grades that both involve bullies.

The first had to do when several of the bullies, the big boys, sought to play a trick on *Herr* Intemann, the teacher who preceded *Herr* Kunzendorf. He had a strong stick about a yard long and used it generously, especially on them. One day after school, they took his stick without his knowledge. They made very fine circular slits, rubbed onions into those slits, and heated the stick so that it became very dry and brittle. Of course they returned it to its proper position before the next school day. Typically, these "big bully" boys misbehaved and were prepared to receive a few flays. No sooner had two or three hits landed on one of the boy's back than a piece of the stick flew off, then another and another. This totally surprised our teacher. He just could not believe what was happening. The boys complained vociferously of their extreme punishment because pieces of the stick had never before broken off when others were disciplined. After school I saw the tough, big, bully boys laughing so hard that tears came rolling down their cheeks. I wondered how they could find humor in someone's humiliation.

Individually, I also drew the attention of a bully. He would attack on my way home after school by calling me names, trying to rip my rucksack from my shoulder, and throwing stones at me. After I had distanced myself by running faster than he could, I often took refuge at the home of my friend, Heinz Laabs. This was much closer to the school building than my home. I would wait there until the boy had disappeared. Another friend, Helmut Winter, was also quite supportive when the bully pestered me. Fortunately I did not have to put up with the abuse of the bully for long. One day he found some unexploded rifle shells, put them in their stove, and blew up their house. Not only was their chimney and kitchen blasted into smithereens, but their whole house – brick no less – was flattened to a heap of rubble. Not having the maturity or perspective I have now, I figured that a bit of divine justice had taken place. He was sent to a reform school after that and so was out of my hair.

FUN AND WORK OUTSIDE OF SCHOOL

Since sports were not in the school curriculum, I joined a *Sport-Verein*, a multi-sport club, and twice a week I went to the dance hall, where sporting activities took place. I began with gymnastics. My instructor, the son of the community miller, taught the rudiments of gymnastics to about twenty of us. We learned tumbling and the basics of working on the various apparatuses. I swung on the single bar, exercised on the parallel bars, jumped on and off the horse, and tumbled on the mats. Eventually I progressed to where I was chosen, along with a few others, to go to a neighboring sporting club to compete with them. At the club good physical care was stressed, and good health was promised as the path to truth and longevity. My participation was my privilege, my physical gain was my benefit, and my sense of team spirit was my delight.

Though we would have liked to play or practice our sporting skills all the time, the practical, daily tasks of living occupied us children too. Mother helped with the milking at the Hastedts, so after we finished our schoolwork, we had to do chores at home. Each child was assigned a night for soup preparation. When my turn came, I worked out a deal with my sister, Elmire, offering to do her schoolwork if she would do the cooking for me. Schoolwork for me was much easier than cooking. As it turned out, I should have learned more cooking, as this is an area in which I am not very proficient. My sister so benefited from the extra cooking opportunities that she has become a very good cook.

Another task the family shared that I thought was fun and challenging was delivering two newspapers, the *ZEVENER ZEITUNG* and the *HAMBURGER ZEITUNG*. Perhaps this is because, much to my great delight, my uncle Jacob, Father's brother-in-law from the next village, gave me a bicycle, just my size. Mother or my siblings delivered the newspapers on foot to the very close neighbors, but because I had the bicycle, I delivered to those farther away. One delivery had me cross the *Autobahn*, but that was of no concern to me since few cars or trucks came along over any given time period. The greater risk was approaching one particular house. Invariably, a gaggle of geese would be waiting for me. As soon as I got near, the head gander, leading the rest, would come running at me, head down and hissing like a steam engine. He attacked my feet and bit me at times. Having been accosted once too often, I made an extra effort one day to gain enough speed to be able to coast right through the gaggle with my feet raised. I aimed right at the gander and was fortunate enough to ride right over his outstretched neck. He never bothered me after that.

An event that captivated almost every citizen of Gyhum was the May Day Festival. It usually took place the first part of May, in a small pasture just north of the Hastedt farm place, next to the home of the tailor. The main event featured a smooth, very tall pole that was anchored in the middle of the pasture. About half the distance up the pole a ring that was perhaps a yard in diameter was fastened with colorful materials. Prizes were fastened on the ring; among them was a ball about eight inches in diameter. I had my eye on that item, since I did not have a ball of my own. It would be perfect for *Fussball*, soccer. The challenge was in climbing to the height of the waiting ring and the prizes. Would I be able to get that high and then be able to reach out and touch the ball to claim it? I convinced myself that I could.

Many a contemporary peer tried and failed to climb the Maypole. Usually they managed to get half or three-fourths the distance up. A few reached the height of the ring but did not touch "my" ball as their prize. Was I ever glad about that! When my turn to climb the pole came, I asked for some divine help, and with a lot of encouragement from my family and friends and a great deal of effort I managed to reach the ring. Then with extreme effort I reached out and touched the ball. It was really mine now! I just had to wait a few days for the presentation, which would occur in our classroom. My head was full of dreams of playing with this hard earned and well-deserved ball. What fun I would have! I was so excited that I barely remembered we were all to weave the colored streamers around the Maypole when the prizes were all claimed. The youth all gathered around the Maypole forming two circles, one circle facing in one direction, the other in the opposite. Each of us was given a colored strip of material to hold that had been attached to the pole. Then, with music playing, we walked around the pole, singing and forming a neat design with our strips tightly woven around the Maypole.

The summer vacation of three weeks coincided with the infestation of potato beetles. During that time we students spent the morning laboriously picking beetles from the potato plants to keep them from devouring the plants. We went from field to field, where we uncomfortably walked the v-shaped furrows. We were so happy for the breaks to rest our aching ankles and backs. What a difference pesticides make today, eliminating the need for such labor-intensive work.

Naturally, it was planned so that our fall vacation coincided with the potato harvesting time, so this was one *Ferien*, school vacation, not many youth anticipated happily. I was certainly one of them. However, throughout the year I did enjoy eating the potatoes that we worked so very hard to earn. Mr. Hastedt invited Mother and some of the other displaced persons to help the hired laborers pick up potatoes. For this they would each earn a sack of potatoes for the day's work. The job did not require skill, and some would call it backbreaking labor because it required constant bending and lifting. Mother chose me to assist her in this painful, labor-intensive work because I was strong enough and tall enough to help with the lifting. In that way I was able to help her earn our sack full of potatoes.

The harvest proceeded in this manner: two horses pulled a machine having a huge spade like tool, which was lowered into the ground, and then a fork-like propeller whirled and scattered the earth raised by the spade. Of course, the potatoes were scattered along with the earth some distance from their original growing spots. It was up to the *Kartoffel Sammler*, the potato pickers, to find the scattered potatoes. What a labor intensive and painful job it was to fill the *Korbs*, baskets, all day long. But dumping them into the strategically placed wagons proved to be the most difficult job of all since the sides of the wagons were at least six feet high. This took both Mother's and my strength to lift and empty the full baskets. Of course, our backs were already hurting plenty from the constant need to bend over and pick up those many scattered potatoes. Lifting the full basket was almost impossible, even for the two of us. We did not have time to rest because if we did not get the potatoes gathered before the horses returned on the next pass through the field, the machine would cover the potatoes that had already been uncovered and scattered. Always we had to hurry, despite the fact our backs were screaming for rest.

Most of the fuel used for heating our rooms, the cook stove, and the outside bake oven came from dried peat, which was dug each spring from the bogs. Mother did not have to dig the peat, but she did have to take care of it once it was dug if she was to get a share. My brother and I were her helpers. Our job was to cut the pieces of the peat with our spade and then stack it in a manner that allowed air to blow through the stack letting these smaller pieces dry more quickly.

* * *

We rode our bicycles out to the bog. The bicycle track was about two feet wide and next to it were the deep tracks dug into the ground by the steel rimmed wheels of the horse drawn wagons. The trip out to the bog was uneventful, but on the way home I had an accident on the bicycle track and experienced an injury to my knee. In no time Mr. Hastedt arrived, saw what had happened, and quickly tied a relatively clean cloth around my knee to stem the bleeding. He loaded me on the motorcycle and took me to *Herr Doktor* Kubart. After treatment the doctor released me with instructions to stay home from school in bed with no activity for about two weeks.

It was hard for me to be inactive, but thanks to the newspaper and schoolwork the time passed even without a radio, TV, DVD, or other electronic games children have today. The doctor came to see me faithfully, as did friends. One good friend, Harlo, left some American comic books for me to help with the boredom. These had been translated into German from their original English. One comic book had the bad guys ravaging parts of New Mexico, and, of course, the good guys were chasing after them. That night I dreamed I was harassed by the bad guys and ran away. In my sleep I moved so much that I actually flexed my right knee and tore the almost healed wound open again. Consequently the doctor ordered two more weeks in bed for me! When that time finally passed, starting to walk again was like stepping on a thousand biting ants. Recovery was slow.

By the time of the grain harvest in July and August, I was healed. I began to help by driving the horses that pulled the empty wagons out toward the fields where the rye and oats were loaded. About half way there, I would meet a full wagon, we would exchange wagons, and I would bring in the full one.

On one trip out to the field, I had just passed a sawmill near the north edge of Gyhum, when the horse to my left began limping in a way I had never seen before. I was quite concerned about this and was relieved when Mr. Hastedt met me with his full load and noticed the problem. He unhitched the horse and had it limp back to the barn. The veterinarian was summoned, who established that the horse had stepped on a nail, which had caused the horse's pain and my consternation. I learned a great lesson through Mr. Hastedt's example. He explained that there is always a risk whether you are working for someone else or, for that matter, yourself. Things happen that you don't expect. You just need to work through them and hope that your employer will understand. Mr. Hastedt certainly did.

By the fall of that year my knee was healed enough for me to play soccer, my favorite sport. We played it whenever and wherever the opportunity presented itself. One early afternoon we were playing in the yard between the confirmation hall and parsonage. In my favorite position on defense, I happened to get the ball coming right my way and was able to meet it and give it the best boot ever. It was a perfect kick, and I was sure I would score. The ball sailed, and sailed, and crashed - right through the parsonage window. Wouldn't you know the ball and all the glass landed on Pastor Jasper while he was taking his afternoon nap! Thankfully he was not cut, but he was mightily shaken. So was I. How could I not have been able to control the trajectory of the ball better? If only I hadn't been so powerful and kicked it so far. I should have run fast enough to catch or even deflect the fast moving ball before it penetrated the window and landed on the pastor. But instead, I had to face the pastor and then, then, my mother. Oh, the trauma! Oh, the humiliation!

For my part in seeing that the window was repaired, I had to get on my bicycle and take the window frame to the next town, Hesedorf, where the repair could be done. I don't know who paid for the repair. My arm holding the frame, taking it and bringing it back, hurt, but my pride hurt a thousand times more because I was responsible for breaking the window in the first place. Having a forgiving pastor and a forgiving mother helped heal that wounded pride over time.

A MOTHER'S LOVE

There came a time when words were spoken about me in seeming whispers that had me very curious. Finally, after I was not able to discern it on my own, I asked outright about the subject that could not be spoken out loud. I learned it had to do with my future. An organization designed to help displaced people did so by offering adoption opportunities to families who were having difficulty economically in keeping all their children in their own family constellation. Switzerland was one nation among several that had families who were ready to adopt such children. Inquiries concerning my family were made to Mother, and ultimately she would have to respond. The choice as to who that adopted child might be turned out to be me. I did not give it much thought, perhaps because I did not fully grasp what it all could really mean, so I put it out of my mind.

My mother did not deal with this subject so lightly. She never fully revealed to me what all she went through emotionally, spiritually, and practically, but it was a very tough decision for her. Economically this would have been a good decision because she would have had one fewer person to provide and care for. This was extremely significant in light of her dreadfully limited earning power. More than likely I would have been placed with a family of greater means, but there were many unknowns and no guarantees, and she decided adoption was not in my best interest. Although I may not have many worldly goods as a member of her family, she knew I would be loved if I stayed with her. Reflecting on this subject now, I am most grateful and appreciative of Mother's decision.

Mother also made many personal sacrifices we were not aware of until much later. A very significant sacrifice concerned dating and marriage. Since Mother was a young, attractive woman when she was widowed, she was offered many opportunities to date. One offer was very difficult for her to decline. It came from my father's brother, David Hehr. He had just been released from the Russian prison and learned that his wife had left him for another man, a high-ranking German official, leaving him very much alone.

He came to Gyhum, I recall, walking with a strange gait. We learned that while he was in prison in Russia all his toes had frozen and had to be amputated. Walking without their support created the unusual gait. He told Mother that his loss of toes would afford him a significant disability income. He felt this would help Mother, if she would marry him, and her children as well. For several reasons that I do not know, except one, Mother declined his kind offer. She told us later that it came down to the fact that she did not want her children becoming the stepchildren of anyone. Again our hearts were filled with renewed appreciation for our mother's deep concern and love for us.

Despite the many things on her mind and the many tasks she had to do, Mother did all that she could to spend specific time with each of us children. I fondly recall walking, all four of us, Adolf, Elmire, Mother and me, hand in hand, north out of Gyhum. When we were almost to the forest, we turned left past an area that had been excavated for rock, sand, or gravel and into the heather. That lowland was filled with birch trees, wild tall grasses, and many birds. Many families had already dug out their peat, leaving little ponds. The birds were plentiful, but the one that got our attention the most was the cuckoo. We would stop and listen, walk further, and listen again, almost assured that we could see the bird making its regular interval calls.

At other times, Mother would walk with one of us individually to the neighboring village of Hesedorf, where she would purchase a new pair of shoes for us, one child at a time, one pair at a time. She simply could not afford to purchase more than one pair of shoes at any one time. The walk with her, hand in hand, was perhaps as much a pleasure as walking home with our new shoes, which had to last for a very long time. Longer has lasted the love of and for our mother.

Mother was also faithful in our Christian education. We all went faithfully to church in Gyhum just as we had everywhere else we had been. We children went to Sunday School on Sunday afternoons at the Lutheran Church, and in the spring of 1951, I began confirmation instruction as well. It was at about this time that I clearly remember having the inclination to pick up my father's big Bible and read it aloud at home. At times Elmire and Adolf were my very patient "congregation," listening to me trying to manage some of those hard to pronounce names. I would stand on the trunk we had brought from Rheinsberg, pretending I was at a lectern. Of course, at this time I had no idea of what my future would be, but I have no doubt God already knew His plan for me.

AN AUDACIOUS IDEA

In the spring of 1951, when I was ready to leave the primary school, my family learned that because I was a displaced person, I was not eligible for the *Mittelschule,* middle school, located in Zeven, ten kilometers away. If I did not attend *Mittelschule*, I would not upon completion be eligible for *Hochschule*, high school. Several other displaced children and I were not permitted to continue our education even though our grades were as good or better than those of some of the children from Gyhum. My formal education was at an end. This was a big disappointment for our family, especially Grandfather.

Grandfather had apparently been thinking about it while he was working with other men chipping mortar off bricks from buildings damaged by the bombs six years earlier. Conditions were still so bad in Germany that it was necessary to reuse damaged building materials. That day Grandfather was injured by a piece of mortar that flew into his eye, causing him immense pain. It was when we were treating his eye that he suggested that our family emigrate and leave Germany. He might as well have thrown one of the bricks he had been cleaning at us! It seemed that we were finally somewhat settled, even though we were considered displaced persons and did not have some of the same rights as other Germans. We had already lived in and been forced to leave Bessarabia, Austria, and Poland. Could or should we leave Germany too? This seemed almost too preposterous to consider.

Grandfather had several reasons for his suggestion, and they all ultimately came down to the fact our schooling was at an end if we stayed in Germany. He used himself as an example, and we could see his humiliation as he spoke. He had had a large amount of land both in Bessarabia and in Poland, from which he made a good living as a farmer. Now the only work he could find was cleaning bricks, and he was paid in butter and milk, not even in currency. By contrast his youngest brother, Rudolf, was working in the *Postamt*, the head postal office of Hamburg. He was comfortable, had enough food, received a salary, and was even purchasing a Volkswagen. He was able to qualify for that comfortable, well-paid position in Hamburg because he had been educated in business in college and had had previous experience in the post offices in Bessarabia. Grandfather thought it was very important that I should study well and be educated too so that when I needed to leave a place, I could take my job with me wherever I was forced to go. Good and free education was available for all children in America, even for immigrants, he assured us.

After World War II, the German economy, like most of Europe, was in a depressed state. Life for most of the people we knew was difficult and desperate. The future seemed very gloomy. Although the Marshall Plan was in place and time proved it to be very successful in changing the economic situation of Germany, it did little initially for the displaced families who had landed in the small rural communities. Many such families had already chosen to emigrate to the USA, Brazil, Argentina, or Canada as a means of escaping the economic hardships and lack of immediate adequate formal education for their children. Grandfather asked, "Adele, what kind of a future will you have if you stay here, where no paying jobs are available to you? And what kind of future will your children have? Adele, you and your children must consider this idea of emigrating. You must not squander their talents. Remember what Jesus said about using your talents to be of help to others. How can your children do that if they are not educated?" Grandfather used every argument he could think of to be persuasive.

If word travels fast in a small village, it must travel even faster within a house occupied by three families. The Lord directed Mr. Rosenow to share his experiences with Mother on the subject that was now the focal point of our thoughts and prayers. Some years ago Mr. Rosenow had lived briefly in the United States in Washington and Oregon. He confirmed Grandfather's advice. He spoke highly of the opportunities in jobs and in education, subjects that were of profound interest to us. Had his wife not died there and his loneliness gotten the better of him, he would never have returned to Bessarabia. There he found his second wife, and despite the whole burden of fleeing, he said he was glad he had returned and had a very dear companion to share his life. Loneliness had disappeared since his second marriage.

In the quiet and sleepless hours of many nights Mother prayed and considered Grandfather's suggestion of emigration and Mr. Rosenow's glowing information about the land "flowing with milk and honey." Should she or should she not heed their caring directives and undertake this enormous task of leaving once more? Could she leave her parents, siblings, extended family, and friends behind and take her children to a far off, unknown place? Would she be able to manage alone with four children? "Please, Lord, help me with this decision. Without your guidance, I shall surely fail."

On the other hand, I had few qualms about leaving Germany and immigrating to another country, maybe to the United States. I had tuned in to all the economic positives of life somewhere abroad, and I envisioned bringing back to my friends and all the youth of Gyhum suitcases full of soccer balls, and if not soccer balls, then at least tennis balls.

Even the thought of leaving the burgeoning Boy Scout chapter did not dampen my enthusiasm. In the spring of 1951, an effort was made to organize a Boy Scout chapter with our teacher, *Herr* Kunzendorf, as the tentative leader. I recall "marching" north out of Gyhum toward and into the forest, where he began to teach us about outdoor living. As much as I enjoyed and would have profited by scouting, I knew I could be marching off to a far bigger adventure and greater opportunities.

Lutheran Church in Gyhum, where Horst began confirmation classes under Pastor Jasper's instruction.

Horst, Elmire holding cousin Renate, Adolf, and cousin Reinhard in front.

THE TETZLAFF FAMILY

Front: Horst, Grandfather Tetzlaff, cousin Reinhard Tetzlaff, Grandmother Tetzlaff, sister Elmire, and brother Adolf. Row two: Aunt Anna Marie (Marichen) and Uncle Ernst Tetzlaff, mother Adele Hehr, Aunt Klara holding Renate and Uncle Friedrich (Fritz) Trautwein. Row three: Aunt Nelly Tetzlaff, Uncle Johann Tetzlaff, Aunt Elfriede Tetzlaff, and brother Friedrich.

The Hehr family: Mother, Adolf, Elmire, Horst and Friedrich. This picture was sent to prospective sponsors in the United States prior to immigration.

ALL THINGS WORK TOGETHER

Grandfather, an avid listener to the radio news broadcasts, heard that the USA was aiding the displaced peoples from Eastern Europe to immigrate. Only two qualifications were needed: excellent health and a sponsor. Lutheran World Relief and Lutheran World Action were two of the agencies that would aid in locating sponsors in the USA. No sooner had Grandfather heard this than he reported to Mother. She was amazed at the timing of this offer, indeed, of the offer itself. It seemed God was at work confirming His will for her.

Then reality set in, or perhaps it was the devil in the guise of doubts, and Mother wondered, "Is our health sufficient? Will anyone consider sponsoring me, a widow, with four children?" With that came more questions and doubts, "What kind of language do they speak anyway? Will I be totally lost? Can I manage on my own away from my parents, from my siblings? Since I did not attend school past the fourth grade because I had to help on the farm, how can I fill out the many complicated legal papers? How can I manage without Klara, who has always helped me with such things?" Yet with Grandfather's encouragement and Klara's help Mother did fill out the proper papers for emigration. Now there was nothing to do but wait. Mother told herself that nothing would ever come of it and thus lessened her anxiety level somewhat.

But, after much, much waiting and praying something did come of it. One day a huge car pulled in to the Hastedt's farm place. It was an American car, a Chrysler. I was totally awed with the size, especially when compared with the German Volkswagen. Several men got out of it and went inside to see Mother. I believe Aunt Klara was there, too. What they said and what Mother responded I never learned. But I was sure this was another step forward in the process of emigration. My excitement raised another notch.

Now there came another decision. In addition to the United States, Canada, Brazil and Argentina, Mother learned that Paraguay, Australia, and France were also now inviting the displaced to immigrate. When our God fills our cup, it truly "runs over." Now Mother had to decide to which country she would apply. She prayed, listened, and decided. Soon she announced the most appropriate place for her and her four children to immigrate would be to the USA, especially in light of Mr. Rosenow's counsel. She knew in her very soul that this was God's will for her and the rest of us.

*   *   *

The Lord tells us that he will never leave us or forsake us. He certainly did not forsake Mother. Shortly after choosing the USA as our destination, Mother received a written message, the directive that we were to go to Hamburg for our thorough physical examinations. In Hamburg we were quartered in army barracks, and each day for two weeks some part of our personage was examined. Many families, we noticed, would come back to the barracks most distraught; their health qualification had not been met. Someone in their family was too sick for their chance to emigrate. We kept wondering, waiting, and praying. What will the final evaluation for each of us look like? Would our health meet the qualifications?

As the days passed, it seemed we were passing more and more tests. Then came the test for TB. Each of us passed except one. One of my siblings needed more examinations to see precisely what his lungs were really like. TB had been in his life, and his body had dealt with it, but was that enough? Upon additional examination the doctor told us that the TB bacillus had been encapsulated with a thick layer of calcium that most likely would never allow the bacillus to spread and cause him or anyone else any harm. My, was that good news! Mother would never have left any one of us behind. She would have chosen to stay with all of us together in Germany. We thanked God that the health criteria for all of us were reached, if only by a squeaky margin.

Now the second criterion, finding a sponsor, needed to be met. Would anyone be willing to sponsor a widow with four children, some who were not yet in their teens? Would the Lutheran Church help us in this task? We were told it was necessary for us first to attempt to find our own sponsor. Every effort was to be made by Mother and relatives in Germany to determine if any relatives living in the USA, or even Canada, would sponsor us. Their responsibility would be to provide employment and housing for a two-year period, thus avoiding dependence on welfare programs within the USA or Canada. We were very much hoping to find a sponsor in the USA.

With much searching, Mother located a cousin of my father, who was living in Alberta, Canada. We were not sure if he would be able to sponsor us if we were to go to North America. And if he were able, would he be so inclined? After our enquiry, he graciously declined, telling us that there were several families asking him to sponsor them. He said if he were to sponsor us, he would feel an obligation to sponsor all those others too. This would to be far too much for him. He declined our request although legally he could not sponsor more than one family in any two-year period.

With his refusal we were back to square one looking for a sponsor. No sponsor, no emigration. Both good health and a sponsor were needed. Then came the letter from Lutheran World Relief informing us that their agency would aid in finding a sponsor for us. Again we had hope because the Lord has a long arm, able to reach across the Atlantic Ocean to find us a suitable sponsor. We had experienced His help throughout the process. Why would He abandon us now?

Across the Atlantic, Lutheran World Relief contacted several pastors of the Southern Minnesota District of the American Lutheran Church. Among them was Pastor Inselmann, who was serving St. Paul Lutheran Church in Conger, Minnesota, and Bear Lake Lutheran, in rural Conger. He received a list of three families who needed sponsors. Two of these families were husband and wife. The third on this list was a widow and her four children.

About this time William Beiser and his wife, Phyllis, were conveniently blessed with the opportunity to purchase a farm located three and one half miles south of Conger from his aunt, Christine Martin. The Beisers were members of St. Paul Lutheran Church and shared with their pastor their joy in the purchase of the farm. They told him that in deep gratitude to God for this opportunity, they wanted to do something special for the Lord. Rev. Inselmann just happened to have a list of families needing sponsorship. The list was carefully scrutinized. The two husband and wife pairs, the Beisers reasoned, could better fend for themselves than the third, a widow with her four children, two not yet teenagers. They would need more help. And Fritz, her oldest son at eighteen could be of some help on the farm. This fact seemed to confirm to them the correctness of their decision to sponsor us.

The news for which we had been hoping and praying made its way back to us. Yes, the Lord reached across the sea to the Beisers and guided them to help the widow, Adele Hehr, because she needed help the most. They agreed to house her and her children with them on their newly purchased farm and to provide employment for two years. Back in Germany we rejoiced to hear this truly good news. The preparations for emigrating were back in full swing.

Part of our preparation for going to America was to learn some English since none of us knew a single English word. Mother approached *Herr* Kunzendorf, our teacher who had taught the upper grades in the elementary school, about tutoring me in English, reasoning that as I learned, I could then teach the others. *Herr* Kunzendorf privately taught British English, but English it was just the same. He agreed to teach me until he learned that we would be going to the United States. Then he forcefully declined. Were we to go to Canada, he would be willing to teach, but not if we were going to America. His hatred for the USA, we later learned, was rooted in his Nazi philosophy. Exactly how he translated his hatred into despising America we could never fully grasp. But because of it my chance to learn English before we went to America was now at a standstill. His hatred for America was so strong that after I was in America and sent a picture of my USA class to him and my former classmates, he told them that we had immigrated to Canada, even though my address and my note with the picture proved differently.

Again, as before, almost all of our belongings gained in the six years while in Gyhum and the precious items we had brought with us so far, even the blanket from the loom of Great-grandmother, had to be weighed by their value and size. We were limited to a wooden trunk (with that blanket inside) and a single suitcase for each of us. Obviously, again much was left behind. Some items Mother could sell – like the peat we had stored for heating and cooking, but most items she simply gave away. But the most important things, her children and family keepsakes, were included for immigration to the USA.

LEAVING EUROPE FOR AMERICA

December 2, 1951, was a momentous day. We took a train to Bremerhaven, where the ship assigned to take us to the USA was docked. The ship, *General Sturgis*, and others had brought American soldiers to Germany and would now in a convoy take displaced people on the return trip to America. The ship was fairly small, only 13,000 tons displacement, while the "mother ship" was about twice this size. We had some distant relatives going to the USA on that ship who later told us this detail and about an interesting event that occurred while they were on the ocean.

As we were boarding, we were told that men and women would be quartered separately. But before we went down to our berths, we looked back to the train on which we had come. Much to our surprise we saw Grandfather and *Tante* Elfriede, Mother's second youngest sister, who had come on another passenger train to bid us farewell. They could not come with us onto the ship, and we could not go back down, so our *auf Wiedersehen* had to be done by waving and by very loud voices. We were so very pleased that they made the extra effort to come and give us one more chance to connect for what could be the very last time.

My sister, Elmire, began to feel nauseous as soon as she stepped onto the ship; she remained so all the way across the Atlantic Ocean. Mother, on the other hand, was not seasick a single day or even an hour. Her sons, however, Fritz, young Adolf, and I were all seasick at least one day of our ten-day journey. The fish were well fed.

After finally finding our "men only" area we chose our berths. There were at least four cots one above another. We wanted to make sure that the person using the top cot was the least likely to send anything down to those in the cots below. Fritz received the honor of occupying the top one. In the women's quarters Elmire had the lowest cot, and Mother had the one just above her. Only during the day could we be with Mother and Elmire; however, not even then could we enter the sleeping quarters of the women and vice versa. That was *Verboten*.

Slowly, ever so slowly, did our ship leave Bremerhaven. We watched Grandfather and Aunt Elfriede receding into the distance, and finally they were no longer distinguishable to our eyes. Perhaps tears caused our visual problems as much as the distance.

We went back down to our sleeping quarters, opened our suitcases and organized for sleep when nighttime would come. When we went back on deck, we began to see to our north an amazing sight rising above the water. It was totally white. We were told we were in the English Channel and were beginning to see the White Cliffs of Dover. What a beautiful sight grew before our eyes, almost like a stage, significantly rising straight out of the waters and very level at the top, with little cars driving, little houses sitting, little trees, well, you get the picture.

Our ship slowed to a halt, and we noticed a uniformed official about to leave our ship along with what we were told was a briefcase of letters. Approaching our ship was a boat that took this uniformed official. It bounced mightily in the waters of the English Channel because of the active waves, but our ship seemed to be totally still. The official left, and the briefcase went with him. Only then did our ship begin to move westward. The sight ahead appeared ominous. If ever one has seen dark, very dark, tumbling clouds coming at you, you have an idea of what we saw. Was this a sign of things to come? Was it a bad omen? We wondered, we prayed.

Back down again we went, Fritz, Adolf, and I. The evening meal was available in the men's mess hall. Each table had a high ridge around it as a retainer for possibly moving tableware. In the middle of each table was a pole, which reached from the floor to the ceiling and could be used for stabilization in rough weather. The meals were tasty, delicious, and plentiful. When the ship was bounced around by the high waves so common in the Atlantic Ocean, our dishes slid from one end of the table to the other, but not off, caught by that significant ridge. Not only was the tableware upset when we had rough waves, but also for many of us, our stomachs.

We were introduced to new foods. Peanut butter was one such item. It had a most unusual smell and tasted so different, but the most challenging part was trying to get it off the roof of the mouth. It stuck like glue. Peanuts themselves were new too; they were not like the nuts with which we were acquainted. We found it extremely strange that corn was set before us to eat. In Europe corn is fed to animals, yet, here it was served to humans - the audacity. All these and several other American dishes I came to accept with time, and then appreciate, even to long for as part of my diet.

Since my brother, Fritz, had already been a full-time farm hand at the Hastedt's farm, he was now required by the Lutheran World Action Agency to work on the ship. His assignment was to work in the kitchen. He told of huge buckets of unrefrigerated cracked eggs that we suspected had a way of contributing to our great stomach discomfort.

Fritz was informed by some of the fellow kitchen workers that he should reconsider going to the state of Minnesota. "Why, there are wolves on the loose, the roads are no more than mud tracks, the homes are still without indoor plumbing, etc., etc." When he shared the warnings with the rest of us, we began to believe them. They gave us something to ponder as we slowly crossed the Atlantic. We wondered where indeed our dear mother, with God's gracious help, was about to take us. We would certainly want to ask some questions to check out this information once we arrived in Minnesota.

As we traversed the ocean, many sea gulls followed our ship, both day and night. We also realized fish were accompanying us. We could see them as they leaped from the middle of one wave, only to disappear in the next one. Why were the fish and birds following us? Were they feeding on what was dumped into the ocean? One can only guess.

*   *   *

Three days before New York we encountered the nasty part of the Atlantic Ocean. The warm waters of the Gulf of Mexico buffeting the cold, northern waters of the Atlantic created severe traveling conditions. The waves and the winds together began to rage as we had not encountered before. Decks C and B were locked and off limits. Only deck A was high enough to avoid the powerful waves rushing across the ship from stem to stern. They were so high that the comparison was made to a house, indicating the waves were about two stories high. That caused our small ship to ride two waves and then plunge mightily into the third giving the ship profound shivers. We compared the shaking to what we imagined a giant would cause with a huge hammer if he pounded on the ship every so often, giving the ship and us the shakes and penetrating even into our very souls. As land lovers, we had had no idea that such severe weather rages in the great oceans. But, we reminded ourselves, God is mightier than any ocean.

*   *   *

The next day, two days from New York, with the waters a little less tumultuous, a loud announcement came telling all persons on our ship to go up on decks A, B, and C and put on our orange life vests. It took a while for us to get the message because it came in a language that was still foreign to us. Finally the meaning of the message was passed along to everyone. We were all on our several decks when we realized that we were turning around; our ship was facing the direction we had come. Since we did not know the reason for this strange development, many speculated on the reason for the turn around. Was it a drill? Were they going to take us back to Germany because someone had done something terribly bad? Only later did the reason become clear.

*   *   *

The details, later described by our distant relatives who were on the mother ship a day behind us, made sense of our strange activity. Their ship had encountered those same fierce winds and two-story high waves too. But their ship happened to land on two extremely high waves in such a way that one huge, high wave was located at the ship's very front, one wave was at its very rear, and very little water was under the ship's center. This lack of support caused the ship to break in its center. It took on water, sirens were sounded, and other ships were called for possible rescue operations. That is why we turned around, ready to offer help.

By design, most ships, especially those designed to transport people, have their lowest two levels inside as enclosed empty rooms. Should the outer shell, though made of thick steel, somehow be penetrated, those lower empty rooms would fill with water, but not add more water into the remainder of the ship. The ship could still remain afloat. The hope, of course, is to seal the opening. The mother ship had experienced that tear in its underside. One can picture it by thinking that it was hung up by its ends, and its sheer weight, not supported in the center, broke open.

95

With time our ship again turned westward, we were allowed to remove our life vests, and all seemed as normal as one would expect. Of course we were unaware of the reason for the delay and of the "interesting" repairs that were made on the ship on which our relatives were quartered. The ingenious repair ratcheted together some cables, which had been attached inside just above the steel hull, bringing the separated parts of the hull closer together. Then pieces of steel were welded – under water no less – into those openings, allowing the ship to "limp" into New York harbor. Once the repairs were made, our ship and others on alert were free to turn westward. The need to rescue passengers from a sinking ship was averted.

The barracks in Bremerhaven, Germany, where the Hehr family stayed just prior to embarking on the ship for America.

USNS *General S. D. Sturgis*, the troop transport that brought the Hehr family to America.

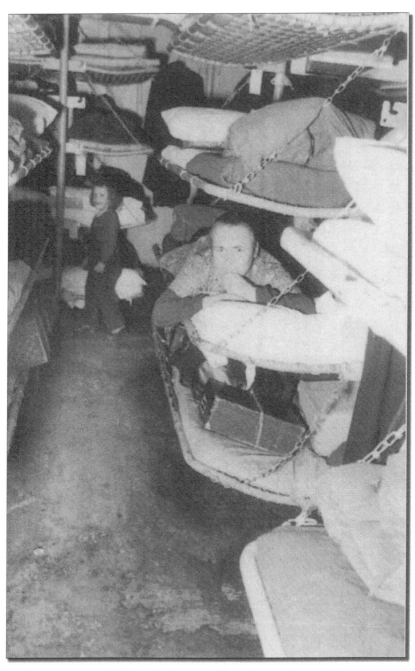

Adele Hehr on her berth in the ship.

Böck II. Zimmer 70

Schwer- / Hand- Gepäck

Verzeichnis

Transportnummer
Laufende Nr

Über mitgeführtes D.P.-Auswanderungsgut, enthaltend die im rechtmäßigen Besitz befindlichen persönlichen und Haushaltsgegenstände der

1.
2. Ausfertigung
3.

NAMEN: H e h r , Adele

D.P.Nr: 519 211   Nationalität: Deutsche   ZIEL (Staat) U. S. A.

Ich beantrage zollamtliche Abfertigung und erkläre, daß in den vorgeführten Gepäckstücken nur die aufgeführten Gegenstände in denselben verbotenes Eigentum enthalten sind.

Befugnis zur Ausfuhrbewilligung vom ..... Nr. .....

Gepäckstück Nr. 3 Koffer Wert 156,- DM	Gepäckstück Nr. 4 Koffer Wert 201,- DM	Gepäckstück Nr. 5 Koffer Wert 434,- DM	Gepäckstück Nr. 5 Koffer Wert 434,- DM
2 Oberhemden	5 Höschen	3 Unterhemden	6 Taschentücher
4 Unterhemden	4 Hemden	3 Unterhosen	1 P.Turnschuhe
1 Turnhemd	2 Unterkleider	2 Turnhosen	1 Besteck
4 P.Unterhosen	3 Schlüpfer	1 Turnhemd	1 Schuhlöffel
1 Hosenträger	5 P.Strümpfe	1 Album	1 Stück Seife
1 Weste	1 P.Hausschuhe	1 Herrenjacke	1 P.Herrenschuhe
2 P.Strümpfe	2 P.Socken	6 P.Socken	1 Schal
1 P.Knabenstiefel	2 Nachthemden	1 Herrenanzug	1 Trainingshemd
2 P.Kniestrümpfe	1 Weste	1 Knabenanzug	
2 Handtücher	1 Nähkasten	1 Weste	
1 Schlafanzug	1 Schal	5 Oberhemden	
1 P.Socken	1 P.Sandalen	2 Handtücher	
1 Trainingshose	2 Handtücher	1 Mundharmonika	
1 Löffel	3 Schürzen	1 Rasierk.m.Inh.	
1 Teller	1 Bluse	5 Krawatten	
1 Zahnbürste	Tasse,Zahnbürste	1 Schlafanzug	
6 Taschentücher	6 Taschentücher	1 Hosenriemen	
1 Tasse	2 halbe Röcke	1 Tasse	
1 P.Turnschuhe	1 Kleid / 6 Kaffeelöffel	1 Zahnbürste	

Ich erkläre hiermit, daß ich den Inhalt dieses Formulares dem Antragsteller in ... Sprache vorgelesen habe und daß er bestätigte, den Inhalt verstanden zu haben

Unterschrift: Adele Hehr

Zollamtlich abgefertigt
Zollstelle von hier Nr
Zollsbfertigungsstelle:
Wentorf A.W.

Bitte in GROSSEN DRUCKBUCHSTABEN und in deutscher Sprache ausfüllen

Declaration of items brought onto the ship - Page 1.

99

Schwer }
Hand } Gepäck

Verzeichnis

Transportkt. Nr.

Laufende Nr.

1.
2. Ausfertigung
3.

über mitgeführtes D.P.-Auswanderungsgut, enthaltend die im rechtmäßigen Besitz befindlichen
persönlichen und Haushalts-Gegenstände der

NAMEN   M e h r , Adele

D.P. Nr.: **519 911**   Nationalität: **Deutsche**   ZIEL (Staat): **U. S. A.**

Ich beantrage zollamtliche Abfertigung und erkläre, daß in den vorgeführten Gepäckstücken nur die aufgeführten
Gegenstände, insbesondere kein verbotenes Eigentum enthalten sind.

Beigefügt ist: Ausfuhrbewilligung vom   Nr.

Gepäckstück Nr. 6	Gepäckstück Nr. 6	Gepäckstück Nr. 5.	Gepäckstück Nr. 5.
Art. **Koffer** DM	Art. **Koffer** DM	Art. **Koffer** DM	Art. **Koffer** DM
Wert **214,-**	Wert **214,-**	Wert **202,-**	Wert **202,-**
Der gold.Schnitt	12 Haarspangen	1 Album	1 Blockflöte
3 P.Strümpfe	1 Kopfband	2 Turnhemden	1 Trainingsanzug
2 Nachthemden	1 Löffel	2 Oberhemden	1 Teller
1 Kleid	1 Teller	2 Unterhemden	1 P.Turnschuhe
3 Hemden	1 Trainingshose	4 P.Unterhosen	
4 Schlüpfer		2 Westen	
2 Unterröcke		2 P.Kniestrümpfe	
2 Schürzen		1 P.Socken	
1 Jacke		2 P.Strümpfe	
1 P.Schuhe		1 Hosenträger	
2 P.Kniestrümpfe		1 Knabenanzug	
2 Handtücher		2 Handtücher	
1 P.Socken		1 Schlafanzug	
2 halbe Röcke		1 Atlas(Western)	
2 Kleider		1 P.Knabenschuhe	
2 Pullover		1 Löffel	
1 Tasse		1 Tasse	
1 Zahnbürste		6 Taschentücher	
6 Taschentücher		1 Zahnbürste	

Ich erkläre hiermit, daß ich
den Inhalt dieses Formulars
dem Antragsteller in
Sprache vorgelesen habe und
daß er bestätigte, den Inhalt
verstanden zu haben.

Unterschrift: *Adele Mehr*

Zollamtlich abgefertigt
Zollbleie von hier Nr.
Zollabfertigungsstelle
Wentorf A.W.

Bitte in GROSSEN DRUCKBUCHSTABEN und in deutscher Sprache ausfüllen.

Declaration of items brought onto the ship - Page 2.

ARRIVING IN AMERICA

On the evening of December 13, 1951, eleven days after we had left Bremerhaven, we began to see lights. Soon there were more, and then even more. I had never ever seen so many in all my life. In Germany during the war only one light bulb was used in our living quarters, and we transferred it from one room to another for light when the electricity was on. All too often the electricity was off, and we had no light at all. We were astounded at the multitude of lights greeting us as we arrived in America! What a contrast!

The evening turned into night, but nobody on the ship seemed to want to sleep. There was so much to see. As we came closer and closer to the lights, we saw a statue of a very tall lady with a light at the top of her right arm, which she had stretched up high. She was standing there almost in the middle of the New York harbor. Later I learned that we had seen the Statue of Liberty, given to the USA by France and dedicated on October 28, 1886. It is meant to be a sign of welcome to all. A poem by Emma Lazarus found in the base of the statue states, "…give me your tired, your poor, your huddled masses, yearning to breathe free, the wretched refuse of your teaming shore. Send these, the homeless, tempest- tossed to me. I lift my lamp beside the golden door." We certainly qualified for the welcome. We slept little that night, excited by what we were seeing and also from the anticipation of everything we would soon be experiencing in our new, chosen country.

The next morning, December 14, 1951, our ship anchored at Pier 42. The sun was shining. Many people were already disembarking by the time Fritz, Adolf, and I, with suitcases in hand, located Mother and Elmire. We approached the gangplank and disembarked together as a family. America, here we come!

Looking down, one of the first things I saw on American soil was a tall person in a dark blue, almost black, uniform. This immediately reminded me of how the German SS soldiers dressed. My thoughts raced. "Does America have those feared and ugly SS people too?" I cringed at this possibility. "Why did we travel all this distance only to be hounded by evil people here too? We should go right back to Germany. At least there the SS had been eliminated after Hitler's demonic reign had come to its proper end. Why are they here at the harbor?" My head and heart spun with questions and fear.

The gangplank from ship to shore was not that long, but the disembarking passengers on it moved very slowly, making it seem very long. When our snail-paced queue finally brought us down closer to the SS person, new questions surfaced because the SS person appeared to be different. "Can it be a woman?" I wondered. "Has America become so desperate that their SS people are women too? Do the women SS in America get only one S to show a lesser rank?" As I got closer, I was sure this was a woman. "The Nazi SS in Germany were never women," I concluded, according to my limited knowledge. Just as I was realizing this, I realized there was something else very different. The S woman was smiling and offering something to each person coming ashore. It was a doughnut. "The Nazi SS

102

never gave anything except rude orders and, sometimes, harsh curses," were my thoughts. With mixed feelings I accepted her gracious gift. I found I had more to "chew" on than just the doughnut.

Later I learned that the woman whom I, and hundreds of others, met was from the church called the Salvation Army. That accounted for the uniform and the one letter S. Their mission of ministering to others is squarely based on the name of Jesus Christ, who teaches ministry "even to the least of these." And at that time our displaced family carrying all we owned in our suitcases, would have, if asked, agreed we were members of the group that qualified as "the least." The doughnut left a sweet taste in our mouths. It became a sign of many more great things to come our way in our new welcoming, accepting, chosen country. We felt privileged to enter.

IMMIGRANTS IN AMERICA

From the harbor room in a huge, tall building with equally huge, high, windows, we looked into New York City. Two things jumped out at me. First, I could not miss the tall, super tall, buildings in all directions. But what I noticed next was just overwhelming to me altogether. Cars, cars, and still more cars. Just below the window where I was standing, there was a multilane road. In each lane were cars, one after another. How I longed to have a chance to ride in one someday. When we were in Gyhum, we could walk to the *Autobahn*, half a kilometer away, sit on the grass on the side of the ditch, and wait for a vehicle to come by. Our wait was often five to ten minutes and then finally a car came, or maybe a truck. How different this was!

Fascinated by the sheer number of vehicles, my curiosity soon shifted to how these cars worked. What made them move? There was no obvious means of locomotion. They had no horses, no one was pushing, they just moved. Some moved rather fast too. Why the difference? What did one have to do to get these things to move faster or slower, to stop, or even beep? I was eager to learn the answer to these questions in this super many auto land of America.

My contemplation was interrupted, and we were ushered outside. Before I knew it, we all were actually getting into one of these yellow autos with the name "taxi" on its top. I could hardly believe that I was really inside one of these cars I had been watching out the window. Awesome! We all sat behind the driver, some of us facing backward and others facing forward. I could not see much of what the driver did. But, whatever he did, his taxi moved into traffic. Swiftly it went in and out of lanes, stopping at the red lights that were on posts of some streets. The taxi driver managed so efficiently and speedily that we arrived at our destination safely and far too soon, in my opinion. Our destination, the Grand Central Railway Station, was huge, impressive, and glorious to this inexperienced German boy. We were accompanied from the harbor to the station by a German speaking representative of Lutheran World Relief. She helped us find the train we would take to that unknown state called Minnesota, where Mr. Beiser, from Glenville, Minnesota, would come to pick us up.

This was some train. Our trains in Germany had wooden seats, were very noisy, and went very slowly. They produced voluminous dark smoke and let off lots of steam. The American train, by contrast, ran so very quietly and smoothly, traveled much faster, and did not give off that nasty smoke and steam. It even had cushioned seats that leaned back! Traveling on the train with us were several other immigrant families as well as the nice Lutheran World Relief representative. She gave us all brown bags that had sandwiches and milk. While speaking in pretty good German, she updated Mother on some things I did not understand or even care about. I was glued to the huge train window framing my first pictures of America.

*   *   *

The huge city of New York was left behind and the countryside was there to behold. Something was different about this "countryside." Quite often I saw what seemed like very small villages that had a house, some barns, a round high tower – almost like castles in Germany - usually with trees surrounding it, and a lot of fences. What I did not understand was the purpose and the smallness of what I thought were the many small villages. They were in sheer contrast to the super tall buildings of the huge city of New York and the other large cities through which we traveled.

The representative from Lutheran World Relief informed us that we were about to enter the state called Pennsylvania and soon thereafter we would encounter a "blizzard." We never had a blizzard in Germany, perhaps in Bessarabia, but I was too small to remember anything like that. Perhaps we encountered a blizzard when fleeing, but I am not sure. She said it was probable this severe snowstorm would delay our arrival at the railroad station in Minneapolis by about an hour. But, she added, we would gain that lost hour back when we crossed into the Central Time Zone near Chicago. America was so big that it had two time zones? We would leave the Eastern Time Zone and enter the Central Time Zone. That was something to ponder. We would lose an hour and then we would regain an hour. It seemed more than fair, don't you agree?

We traveled all day, through the night, and most of the next day. Finally at dusk on December 15, the train pulled into the railroad station in Minneapolis. It seemed as big as the huge railroad station where we had started in New York City. As we disembarked from the train, we noticed the snow, ice, and terrible cold. It was a big contrast to the pleasantly comfortable temperatures inside the train. We were noticed too. Standing several yards off was a gentleman who smiled and motioned us to come. We came. He shook our hands and with some pretty good German identified himself as William Beiser. This was the man who had agreed to be our sponsor. We were so very pleased that he knew some German because none of us knew any English. Sometime later he shared that he had no difficulty recognizing us. Our strange looking clothing and our confused facial expressions had given us away.

What followed also pleased us. Mr. Beiser invited us to come with him into a huge, chandeliered dining room. There, a large table was already set for dining. The sandwiches we had received on the train were nice, but they did not satisfy the hunger of a growing thirteen year old boy. We sat down with Mother sitting at the opposite end of the table from where I sat. Before our delicious meal arrived, Mr. Beiser smiled, bowed his head, and said words that seemed very nasal sounding. Mother winked at me. We then all bowed our heads, and I wondered if he was praying, and if he was, could God understand his words? I surely did not. Later, I asked Mother what she meant by winking at me. She said that if Mr. Beiser was praying, it must surely be to the same God who had been our strength and protection, our adviser, and the source of all good gifts and sufficient grace to meet our needs. He had gotten us alive and well out of Bessarabia, out of Austria, out of Poland, and now out of Germany, and we would also be cared for by Him in this great land of the United States of America. I concluded God must also be able to understand English prayers, even for the delicious meal He had provided with Mr. Beiser.

Once we had eaten, Mr. Beiser led us up and down stairs and finally to one of many cars in the huge parking lot. We were about to enter a privately owned automobile for the first time. I was so very excited, and I could not wait to get in and hopefully sit in the front seat. Once our suitcases were placed into the huge trunk of the Mercury coupe Mr. Beiser had borrowed to get us, we entered the car. Mr. Beiser sat behind the steering wheel. I sat next to him. My wish was granted! Fritz sat next to me; Mother, Elmire, and Adolf sat in the back seat. We were finally heading to our new home in the "backward" land of Minnesota, as Fritz had so convincingly informed us boys while we were on the ship.

Mr. Beiser did something with some keys, and I heard a purring sound. My excitement grew. He pulled something, and lights came on, bright ones outside, showing us the road ahead, and colored ones in front of him on the dashboard. How nice it would have been to have lights on our wagon when we fled. Traveling at night without lights must have made the arduous trip even more challenging for those who had to determine the route. Thanks to the lights Mr. Beiser could see very well where he was going. He moved a lever, the purring increased, and we were moving. This was all most interesting to me. And, contrary to the predictions on the ship, Mr. Beiser was driving on solid ground, pavement, with snow at our sides, and not on dirt roads.

I looked out at the tall buildings of the city of Minneapolis, but before long I saw only smaller buildings and then only buildings now and then along our way. The snow became higher on the sides of the road. Mr. Beiser asked if we were warm enough. Mother and those in the back seat said they were somewhat cool. He pushed a lever or dialed something. I don't remember exactly what he manipulated, but soon the extra warmth needed in the back seat was coming. Incredible! And he did something more when suddenly there was music soothing our highly anticipatory nerves. What a machine: music, warmth, lights, and movement at speeds up to sixty miles per hour. I was overwhelmed with its reality. Now that I was actually riding in one, I began to hope that maybe, maybe, someday I could drive one of these phenomenal machines.

We drove and we drove, and though I looked, I never did see the prophesied wolves and the dirt roads. Toward the end of our drive, I saw some blond gravel roads, but nothing like the description of Minnesota roads given to Fritz. Praise the Lord! I began to think that perhaps the information about Minnesota was just so much hot (cold) air.

After we left the major highway for a lesser highway and then that blond gravel, Mr. Beiser told us that we had gone through a town called Conger. In our minds this meant little since we had been told that he lived in Glenville, Minnesota. Shortly after leaving Conger, about three and a half miles more, he turned into what we thought was Glenville. It surely seemed small to me. "This must be a very small village," I thought.

The snow was even higher here. It was a clear, moonlit night, and I could see the outline of some buildings over the snow. There was a high round tower, a huge building, several smaller ones and then a white one that we entered. I asked Mr. Beiser if this was Glenville. He smiled and said, "Well, *ja und nein*," yes and no. With that unclear response we entered the Beiser home. There he introduced us to his lovely wife, Phyllis, who met us with a most gracious, welcoming smile and showed us around. Their, now our, home was well lit and pleasantly warm; and, oh dear, yes, it even had indoor plumbing, too, sufficient for all human needs. That we did not have to go to an outhouse was a very special privilege. Mother and the rest of us thanked the Beisers many times for their willingness to share their home with us.

For our accommodations we were given two bedrooms located on the second floor. In Germany we had only one bedroom. Upon its completion, a short while later, we also had a kitchen and living room combination that had the basic appliances and furniture. This first floor room was bigger than any room we had ever had. What gracious gifts, what gracious hosts, what faithful sponsors. Even in later years we continued to be appreciative and often expressed our thanks for their gracious willingness to share their warm, Christian home with all its amenities. May they ever be receiving special blessings from above, even as we receive continued blessings here in our new land.

GETTING ACQUAINTED

In the daylight the next morning I could see the buildings clearly through the windows. I thought that the people of Glenville, in this very small village, surely had a variety of buildings. There was that tower again, a huge, round-roofed building that looked more like a barn than living quarters, several small buildings that seemed more like sheds, not suitable for human dwellings. When Mr. Beiser came into the house, carrying a pail with some milk in it, I again asked him if we were in Glenville. With his gracious smile he explained, "No, these buildings are all a part of my farm." Without thinking, I replied, "Wow, you must be a millionaire to own all these buildings." He smiled and added, "Yes, I own these buildings. Most of the land you see out there, now covered with snow, belongs to this farm, too. In America we farmers live on our land, not in villages like the farmers do in Germany. We do not have to travel to get to the land we chose to cultivate; it is all around our buildings."

As a part of his sponsorship Mr. Beiser had agreed to provide employment so that we would have some income. To fulfill this agreement he had purchased ten milk cows. Mr. Beiser, Mother, Fritz, and I milked these cows. The revenue from the milk was our earnings. Mr. Beiser also employed Fritz as a full-time hired man on the farm. As time went on, he helped Mother find employment cleaning homes, especially that of Mr. and Mrs. Babbitt of Conger.

Since we would not go to school until after Christmas vacation, Mr. Beiser helped to fill the days by teaching some English to us. Compared to German, I thought English sounded very nasal, and the *th* sound was new and challenging. It seemed that Mother had the most difficulty trying to master it. Much later I learned that the *th* sound of the English language and the *ch* sound in the German language are extremely difficult for students of these new languages, especially if they are adults over twenty. At our birth our creator God gives us the tools to make any sound a language ever demands; however, when certain sounds are not produced because they may not be needed in a particular tongue, then those muscles atrophy rendering the person unable to produce those sounds. Thus adult Germans most likely cannot say the *th* properly, and adult English-speaking people can most likely not say the German *ch* sound properly.

When Sunday came, we went to the worship service at St. Paul Lutheran Church in Conger, Minnesota, with the Beisers. The trip itself was like a gift to me. We rode in great comfort of a newly acquired Studebaker Commander, which Mr. Beiser had purchased because his pickup truck was not roomy enough for all of us. We had never traveled to church in such a luxurious manner before. I was ready to go to church every day if the mode of transportation would be the same. Once there we could not understand most of what was said, sung, or preached during the service. Since the congregation had many members who were of German decent and who could speak some German, the experience afterward was a delight because we were able to connect with some in our native tongue.

Many, if not most, of the congregation were surprised that we were there. The Beisers and Pastor Inselmann had kept the news of our coming to the US to a minimum; therefore, we were a big surprise for many of the community.

Because the clothing that we wore coming from Germany was so different (e.g., my short pants and long woolen socks), plans were quickly made to purchase the DP family, as we came to be known, some new clothes. The next day Pastor Inselmann took us to Albert Lea to St. Paul's Clothing Store and bought American style clothing for us. Thank you, Pastor, for taking us to that clothing store. Thank you, congregational members, who provided the money for our American style clothing.

What Elmire, Adolf, and I did not know as we were delighting in our new clothes was there was a "cost" to be paid for them. In return we were to recite German poems and sing German Christmas Carols at the Christmas worship service. This, of course, pleased the German-speaking members of the congregation. Mrs. Schoenrock and her daughter Jane played the electric organ for us. Both were so very talented on the organ and shared their talent willingly. We were pleased to be included, but hopefully even more pleased was the giver of all talents, who intends they be used for His glory.

We spent a good portion of Christmas day at the Christine Martin home in Conger. She is the aunt of William Beiser from whom he purchased his farm. Other guests were Martin and Mable Sherb, sister and brother-in-law to Mr. Beiser, who were quite fluent in German. With us they sang many German Christmas carols and helped us feel more "at home" in this non-German-speaking world. They contributed greatly to making our first Christmas in America very memorable.

THE LONG RECESS IS OVER

After the Christmas vacation, ending very early in January of 1952, Elmire, Adolf, and I started school. We had not been in school since our trip to Hamburg for our physical examinations way back in October of 1951. Our school was located in Conger, about three and a half miles north of the Beiser farm. We went to school outfitted for the much colder Minnesota winter temperatures than we had been used to in Germany. I now had a heavy winter coat, a cap with earmuffs, thick gloves and high boots. We each got a new "lunch bucket," something entirely new to us, since in Germany we had eaten our noon meals at home after we had gotten out of school at one p.m. The school day in Conger ended at three, and we ate our noon meal at school. That made a long day. We were delightfully surprised that the school week lasted only to Friday, which made the idea of the long day more manageable. Having no Saturday classes was marvelous!

Since school buses were not used in those days, we walked straight north, passing the homes and farms of the Ranges, the Behrs, the Lemkes, the Lindemanns, the Wichmanns, the Dreschers, and the Wittmers on the hill. Several small hills made the terrain a challenge, especially when the wind was strong against us coming from the north-northwest wanting to push us back. At times we had mini icicles forming on our faces, but most times in bad weather either Mr. Beiser in his Studebaker or some of the farmers driving to Conger delivering their cream to the Conger creamery took us to school.

These farmers were so very kind to invite us into their warm cars, which traveled much faster than we did by walking. Stranger danger was not an issue in rural Minnesota in 1952. Society then did not seem to have this present evil, but was a trustworthy, caring, honest, loving society. I grieve at the evil developments in my adopted land. Would that America's society again be trustworthy, caring, honest, and loving!

One day much later on our way home from school Adolf and I, Elmire having stayed in Conger with Christine Martin, were invited to ride with our neighbor, Otto Range, who was coming home from work at the Wilson Packing Plant in Albert Lea. He was a kind, gentle man who had given us rides on other occasions. He would take us as far as his home, which was but a tenth of mile from the Beiser farm, and we always eagerly accepted his invitation because we would then have a short walk. Adolf went into the back seat of the 1938 Ford, and I stayed in front, next to Mr. Range.

We headed south, leaving the main, wider gravel road and entered the fairly narrow one that went past his home and on to the Beisers'. This portion of the road has two major hills - at least walking them seemed to make them major. As Mr. Range loved to do, he asked us about school, making eye contact with us for significant periods of time. It seemed the car knew its way automatically, and he did not have to watch his driving. What the car and the gracious driver did

114

not anticipate, however, was the approach of another car coming up the same hill from the opposite side, going north. Two men were in their black car driving up the center of the road north while Mr. Range was driving in the center of the road heading south. Of course, we crashed. Adolf bounced around in the back seat, and I flew forward. My head went into the windshield, and my chin met the rim of the clock located on the passenger's side of the dashboard. Fortunately, both vehicles had been approaching each other at a very slow speed, and damage to the cars was minimal. After the dust had cleared, we assessed damage to ourselves. Adolf appeared fine after some moments of disorientation. I thought I was fine, too, but Adolf and Mr. Range did not agree. They saw me bleeding from my chin. Since I could not see myself, I was surprised to hear there was damage to my face. I felt no pain. No laceration was noted on my head where I hit the windshield, but my chin got it.

Meanwhile, at home while Mother was doing some needlework, she felt a shiver, stuck herself with the needle - a most rare occurrence since she was an accomplished seamstress - and determined in her mind that something must have gone wrong with her children. Shortly, she learned of the accident and concluded that her experience at home and the accident were happening simultaneously. Mother had the gift of sensing intuitively the presence of significant events happening in the lives of her family.

Soon, Mr. Beiser appeared with his car and took me to Naeve Hospital in Albert Lea, where Dr. Schmidt had come from his clinic in Alden to attend to my chin. The crushed nature of my laceration made sewing very difficult, and Dr. Schmidt told that I might have a scar there for life. He was right; I still have the scar, which makes shaving very challenging. I learned early on not to use a razor, for it would always want to take off more than my whiskers. Electric shavers respect the scar and only take the whiskers.

LEARNING THE LANGUAGE

In January of 1952, Elmire, Adolf, and I began our schooling in America at the Conger Elementary School. The teaching staff consisted of two lovely ladies, Miss Ottesen and Miss Madsen. Although we were 12, 11, and 13 respectively, we were placed in the lower elementary classroom with Miss Ottesen as our teacher because of our extremely limited knowledge of English. I am still totally impressed with the courage, the compassion, and the patience Miss Ottesen showed us. Not only did she have four different classes to teach, she had three different, very different students, to teach also. How do you manage? How can you get anything across to them if they do not understand you and continually say, *nichts verstehen*? And how can the students, who may want to learn, get anything educationally from their teacher when they cannot understand her directives and assignments? My hat and heart go out to Miss Ottesen for all her most gracious efforts of teaching my sister, brother, and me despite seemingly insurmountable challenges.

Miss Ottesen used the chalkboard to list vocabulary for us. One day she listed seven words in a way that it was apparent they belonged together. I speculated what seven belonged together, and it occurred to me that they could be the days of the week. *Sontag* looked similar to Sunday, and *Montag* was similar to Monday, but *Dienstag* and *Mittwoch* were nothing like Tuesday and Wednesday. Miss Ottesen asked us to pronounce the words. Of course our German pronunciation was unlike what she expected. When she pronounced them for us, I was surprised, no, shocked, that so many of the letters in the words were not pronounced.

Brilliantly, on her part, Miss Ottesen had me sit next to the *World Book Encyclopedia*, because I did have significant time on my hands, so why not look and see the pictures, try to read beneath them, do something to relate the picture with the writing. She also had other students assist us with beginning reading skills when they had free time. How humiliating it was for me to learn to read about Dick, Jane, Sally, and Spot from students who were close to half my age.

It was humiliating to be taught by younger students, but harder yet was grasping the unusual pronunciations of English words. We were used to a language where each letter had its own particular sound. As a result, learning to read and spell in the German language was much easier because there were few exceptions to the rules. We found that was not the case with the new language we were trying to master. Most letters seemed to have more than one sound or pronunciation, and they were not necessarily the same as those to which we were accustomed. Not only was that true, but some letters were at times silent in words and had no sound at all! What a challenging, confounding language! No wonder I was confused much of the time.

Eventually, I concluded that each word would need to be memorized – both its pronunciation and its spelling. Then I began to make some progress. Another big help was that the articles preceding nouns did not have gender associated with them as they did in

German. How easy it was to use *the* instead of figuring out whether to use *der, die, or das,* the German articles which had their own idiosyncrasies and sometimes inconsistent rules.

Most of the students were extremely kind and helpful but, as is often the case, there were a few who pointed fingers and laughed. It took me a while to learn enough vocabulary to realize that their behavior often had to do with my name. *Horst Hehr* sounds a lot like *horsehair* to an elementary student. The German equivalent words were not at all similar to the English, but I could see the humor in the situation once I was able to discern what it was that they found so humorous. Unfortunately, though, it was difficult until understanding came, and I must confess I did not always respond graciously to their teasing, especially in the first days and weeks. I'm sure Grandfather was happy and proud that I was on my way, learning the language that would enable me to get a good education, but I doubt that he was proud of my behavior.

By the time the fall of 1953 came, I was reading at the third or fourth grade level, and I advanced to Miss Madsen's class. She taught fifth through eighth grades. Now I was in a room with students of my own age, and I was able to compete with them in regular classes, especially in math. I understood most of what I read and what was going on around me, and the initial teasing had long since stopped. It helped, too, that I was able to participate in the typical sporting games with the other boys and that there were others who enjoyed skating on the flooded pond as much as I did in the winter.

In the summer of 1953, we all moved to Conger to a rented home. The Beisers had graciously housed us for nearly two years. Now it was time for us to "make our own way." Mother was fortunate to have a regular ride to her job at the Banquet chicken-processing factory in Wells, Minnesota. This job allowed her to have some health insurance and to begin to pay into the social security system. Our first house was a converted country schoolhouse. We found it quite cold and drafty in the winter, and so we moved to a two-story frame house that more than met our needs. Mother's wages were hardly sufficient to cover all our expenses, and more and more we children found jobs to supplement the family income.

Conger was a typical self-sufficient small town of the 1950's. It had the necessary businesses, the elementary school and St. Paul Lutheran church. The community sponsored free outdoor movies on Saturday evenings in the summer, and I especially enjoyed attending them, using them to augment my language skills to communicate with the kind, gracious residents of Conger.

At St. Paul's I continued the confirmation classes I had begun in Germany and was confirmed by Pastor Inselmann. He was quite helpful to me in class, providing the necessary translations for my still inadequate English. I wonder if he had a glimpse of my future and purposefully chose my confirmation verse, Colossians 3:2: "Set your minds on things above, not on earthly things." After confirmation he continued to mentor me and see that I got opportunities to attend Bible school and a Lutheran leadership camp. He encouraged me to do well in my studies as preparation for college and made such a dream seem possible with God's help. I thank God for his guidance and prayers for me.

GRANDFATHER'S DREAM

In the fall of 1954, I began high school in Albert Lea. I was continuing to fulfill Grandfather's dream for me by taking advantage of the free *Hochschule* education I had been denied in Germany. It was free, and a bus came to pick me up and take me to class! In Albert Lea I was fortunate to have teachers who continued to make the extra effort to help me learn the necessary skills in English I had not yet grasped. With their tutelage I was getting *A*'s and *B*'s and was on the B Honor Roll within a couple of years. My fellow classmates elected me homeroom president, which made me a part of the student council, and as a Junior I was elected class treasurer.

In 1955 Mother moved to Alden. It was closer to Wells, where she worked. Traveling to work with others in the winter on snow covered, icy roads had always been difficult for her. It was good for her to cut down the miles she would have to travel. By this time we children had been spending more and more time with each of the families for whom we had been working. We had essentially been "farmed out," as many youths of the day were, working for room and board and a small wage.

I had been working and staying, first from time to time and then more consistently, with the Wacholz family, who lived east of Conger. I helped with the farm work and did chores, up at five to help milk the thirty or so cows before school, feeding the pigs and chickens, and returning after school to do it all over again before I began my schoolwork. In the summer I helped with haying and other activities. For this I received thirty dollars a month, every other Sunday off, and, in my mind, the "privilege" of being able to drive a tractor - raking, cultivating, disking, plowing or whatever else needed to be done. After I got my license to drive, I also drove their trucks and car from time to time. Unfortunately while backing their car out of the garage one day, I turned too sharply and dented the front fender. It took me a long time to tell Mr. Wacholz of my mistake. It would have been far better had I confessed at the time. I learned the hard way that time makes the telling harder, not easier.

Although I was living with the Wacholzes, I still maintained a relationship with the Beisers. Mr. Beiser hired me to help him during the summer of 1956 when he was building a new house. He designed and built it himself. It was a good experience. I learned many new skills, enjoyed working for Mr. Beiser again, and earned money for needed expenses and college as well.

The experience of driving on the farm and the money I earned at the Wacholzes enabled me to get my license and buy a car of my own, which had been one of my dreams ever since that first taxi ride in New York City. When I had to drive for the license examiner, I was thankful that my older brother, Fritz, had given me the experience of driving on busier roads in his car. These lessons often came when he picked me up to go to a movie on my day off. He had long since left the Beisers and was employed in Albert Lea at Smith and Douglas, a fertilizer company. My first car was a blue 1946 Chevrolet, for which I paid $75. Soon I traded it with another $150

121

for a green 1949 Chevy. How different were the opportunities in America from what I would have had if we had stayed in Germany.

After my sophomore year the school district lines changed, and the area I was living in was no longer in the district for the Albert Lea High School. Fortunately for me and a few other students from the Conger area already attending classes in Albert Lea, the school board granted a waiver, and we were allowed to continue our education in Albert Lea without having to pay tuition. But it meant that I no longer had transportation to school on the bus. The Albert Lea school district gave me the opportunity to transport two other students and myself and to be reimbursed for my expenses. God opened a way for Grandfather's dream for me to continue.

MEANINGFUL TIMES DURING HIGH SCHOOL

In my junior year I was among the group of students who were chosen to take a trip to Washington, D. C. and New York City during Easter vacation. I continue to be thankful that the local Rotary Club paid my expenses. I assume I was chosen because of my background, that this would be a meaningful, learning experience for me. While I still remember the trip by train to Chicago and through the Appalachian Mountains to Washington, what I remember more is seeing the Capitol where the Senate and House meet to enact legislation. While there we sat in on a Senate hearing. I could not help but compare the system in America to that in Germany, which because of its one party system had not allowed dissent and had therefore allowed Hitler to rise and flourish. I was more thankful than ever to be living in a country where not only are there opportunities, but rule is by democracy.

Returning to New York with a few more years of maturity and better language skills was a delight. I was happy to revisit Grand Central Station and remember how I felt at my first visit. It was fun to look over the city from the Empire State Building. The taxis still dominated the streets, and the skyscrapers still stood guard. We saw a Broadway play and other things, but what remains in my mind after all these years is my reaction to the fact that after I inadvertently left a pair of shoes in the hotel room when we left, they were returned to me in Minnesota! What kind of country is this, I wondered, to care enough to return forgotten shoes to one who is not yet even a citizen?

Naturalization came later that year on May 28, 1957, in the United States District Court in Mankato. Mother, Fritz, Adolf, Elmire, and I had read and discussed the materials that had been sent to us - the Declaration of Independence, the Constitution, its amendments, and the Bill of Rights. That day the judge asked us and several other immigrants questions concerning the meaning of these documents. I was asked five questions and fortunately could answer all. How happy we were when Mother, having a limited grasp of English, was asked only this single question, "Do you want to become a citizen of the United States?" This she understood easily and answered eagerly with a big smile. Thus Mother, Fritz, and I were subsequently declared naturalized citizens of the United States of America! Elmire and Adolf, too young, were naturalized the following year.

That summer through the suggestion of Pastor Inselmann and the generosity of the St. Paul congregation, I was able to attend the Leadership Training School at the Lutheran Bible Camp at Onamia, Minnesota for a week. What a tremendous privilege to hear Dr. Marcus Rieke and other interesting speakers lecturing on various Biblical subjects. The subject that "connected" with me had to do with God's call to serve Him in ministry, based on the message from

Isaiah 6:8: "Then I heard the voice of the Lord saying, 'Whom shall I send? And who will go for us?' And I said, 'Here am I, send me!'"

When I returned home, I reported to the congregation of St. Paul Lutheran Church, thanking them heartily for financing the trip and sharing with them my reaction to what I had heard at the camp. First, I compared my life to that of the earth when it has been without water for a very, very long time and has wide, dry cracks; the Bible Camp experience for me was like refreshing, soaking waters that satisfied the very parched land. I also related the call to ministry made by the Lord as reported in Isaiah. I told them how in my heart and soul I sensed my positive response to His call.

During my senior year, I thought often of college. I worked hard at maintaining my grades and tried to determine which college might be best to attend. Miss Berdan, my Latin teacher, recommended Macalester College in St. Paul, and I arranged a visit. As I was contemplating a possible career in engineering, I also considered the University of Minnesota at Mankato but did not visit. I heard of Wartburg College in Waverly, Iowa, a college affiliated with the American Lutheran Church. It was arranged for a relative of Mr. Beiser to take me to the campus for orientation day for high school students. Whether it was the affiliation with the church, the German name, the literature and curriculum, the good feeling I had while visiting, God's guidance, or a combination of all, I'll never know, but I had no doubt at the end of the day that this was the college I wanted to attend. Graduation day from Albert Lea High School on June 6, 1958, could not come soon enough.

That summer after graduation I found employment at Wilson and Company earning more per hour than I had ever earned before. With the small amount of financial aid I was granted from Wartburg for being a member of the American Lutheran Church, the money I had already saved from working for Mr. Wacholz and Mr. Beiser and from driving forklift at the Del Monte canning plant in Wells the previous summer, the promise of a job on campus, and my new "high paying" job at Wilsons, my finances were coming together. It appeared I would be able to pay for my first year at Wartburg and embark on the next step of Grandfather's dream for me. I was beginning to see that Pastor Inselmann was right when he said that the same God who had helped my mother and family in our many and dire needs would also help me in my present and future needs.

Adele Hehr with sponsors Phyllis and William Beiser on the occasion of the 25th anniversary of the family's arrival in the United States.

The Beiser farm, where the Hehr family lived for two years.

Left, Horst at Conger Elementary School.

Miss Madsen, one of two teachers at Conger Elementary School.

Adolf, Elmire, and Horst at Conger Elementary School.

Horst, graduation from Albert Lea High School. 1958.

Horst and Elmire. Confirmation day at St. Paul Lutheran Church, Conger Minnesota.

Pastor Rudolf Inselmann, who confirmed Horst and Elmire.

WARTBURG COLLEGE

That fall of 1958, my mother and brother Fritz took me to Waverly, Iowa, and I enrolled in Wartburg College. Despite the fact that I was fluent in the German language, I had missed out on much of the formal instruction concerning the language and its literature because of our relocation from German school in Poland to German school in Germany to school in the United States, where there was no opportunity to study German. I, therefore, decided to major in German so that I could catch up on what I had missed. To enhance my understanding of the English language, I minored in English. All of this I did under the umbrella of pre-theological studies. I had not forgotten the words of Isaiah.

Wartburg did not forget its promise to me concerning part-time work. Like many other students I found myself working in food service - washing pots and pans! The dishes and silverware were done in a dishwasher, but the large piles of pans were scoured clean by this lowly freshman. Eventually I was promoted to stocking the serving line with clean dishes, and after that I was on the potato peeling detail. During my junior and senior year I was favored with the ultimate food service job of sitting at the end of one of the two lines and checking whether the students passing by had a five or seven day ticket. Since none of them ever carried their ticket, it meant that I had to memorize each student's individual situation. In addition I was responsible for seeing that no one passed through the line twice. Learning the names and situations of the more than 600 students who passed by seemed a daunting task, but I was motivated by the increase in pay – a dollar an hour! And I was not washing pots and pans or peeling potatoes!

Another job seemed especially suited to me. It was in the language laboratory, where my job was to monitor each booth as students would repeat whatever German words they had heard. If their responses were correct, I would listen to the responses made in another booth. If they were incorrect, I assisted the students to pronounce the words correctly. All this activity was done electronically.

Often I spent Christmas vacation on campus helping the staff with projects that were best accomplished when the students were gone. This was usually washing, waxing, and buffing the floors. I sometimes worked off campus as well. I remember going with my roommate to clear snow from the flat roof of a home after a very heavy snowfall. We could not stand on the roof because it was already sagging from the weight of the snow. We were forced to shovel what snow we could reach while balanced high on ladders. Eventually we cleared enough so that we could stand on the roof to finish. That experience convinced me that I would never own a home having a flat roof.

Of course, I worked during the summers as well. I worked at the Wilson packing plant in Albert Lea for two summers. Another summer I worked in Wells at the Banquet food processing plant. And one summer I worked the early shift at the Wilson plant and then worked the swing shift in Wells at the Del Monte pea packing company. This enabled me to meet my tuition fees each year until my senior year. That year I was $100 short, but that's another story.

AN ANGEL ENTERS MY LIFE

Early in my junior year my path crossed with that of a lovely, blue-eyed brunette. Whether it was in chapel, at work in the cafeteria, or on the way to class, we seemed to meet. Soon the meetings were no longer accidental, and we went to these and many other places together. Her name was Jean Engelhardt. *Jean*, of course, means *John* in French, and in German *Engel* means *angel*. *Hardt* equates to *firmness* or *hardness*. I found I wanted to spend more and more time with one who shared the name of Jesus' beloved disciple and who it seemed to me had the nature, as well as the name, of an angel.

Later that fall I met Jean's parents for the first time on a Saturday afternoon at a football game in Shield Stadium on the Wartburg campus. Knowing that Jean's father was a pastor gave me even more apprehension than I might normally have had because in Germany the pastor and his family are given special, high regard. How formal must I be? What would they think of me? Of course, as the visit progressed, I found my fears were groundless, and I was graciously accepted. It helped that Jean's father spoke some German to me, and I realized he was reaching out trying to make me feel comfortable.

With Jean at my side much of the time, my junior year flew by. It is not surprising, therefore, that the following summer on August 9, 1961, I proposed. We were in Albert Lea by Fountain Lake watching the sunset, and after I read her a special poem written for the occasion, I asked her to marry me. I gave her the diamond ring I had purchased with my summer earnings – earnings which would have gone toward my tuition for my senior year at Wartburg had I not determined that she was a better investment for my future. Fortunately I was able to borrow the $100 I was short and continue working toward Grandfather's dream of higher education for me.

Jean, thinking of our future together, put her educational plans on hold and found a job at the Hillcrest Children's Fold in Dubuque. Working with the children kept her days busy, but I found myself missing her more and more. Our separation made my senior year long and difficult. Graduation day June 2, 1962, could not come soon enough, mostly because I knew our wedding day would follow a week later on June 10.

The wedding was held at St. John's Lutheran church in Preston, Iowa, where Jean's father was the pastor. He officiated at the ceremony, and my good friend and language professor, Dr. Tillmanns, from Wartburg, gave the sermon. The bridal party consisted of my good friend from Alden, Minnesota, Larry Glaeske; Jean's twin sister, Joan; my sister and brothers; Jean's brother as soloist; and other relatives and friends.

ON TO ANOTHER WARTBURG

After a short honeymoon trip to the Missouri Ozarks, Jean and I moved to Dubuque, to a small mobile home in the Ace Trailer Court. Dubuque is the home of Wartburg Theological Seminary, where I would continue my theological education. But first I needed to get a job and attend some night classes at the University of Dubuque to complete the few credits I was short for the requirement for my Bachelor of Arts degree from Wartburg College. This I completed, and on August 31, 1962, I received my diploma.

Jean continued working at the children's home that summer, and I did whatever work I could find. Most of the summer I spent atop a ladder painting a lovely huge home owned by the president of the bank. Some nights I joined other seminary students cleaning the country club near the seminary. That fall Jean found a teaching position at a rural school in Dubuque County. We had purchased our small mobile home on contract for $3000 without interest from an area farmer, and Jean's teaching salary made meeting our $25 per month payments and our other financial obligations easier.

My class schedule at the seminary was rigorous, and in addition I worked evenings and weekends doing yard work, cleaning various businesses, and making deliveries. During vacations and summer breaks, I worked at the Borden Ice Cream Company unloading semis and delivering ice cream to area stores in Illinois and Iowa. In fact, I was out delivering ice cream one summer when our son Timothy decided it was time to be born. Jean drove to the plant but was unable to find me since I was still out on the route. She returned home, and a neighbor was able to locate me by phone in time for me to return home and take Jean to the hospital for the delivery. Fortunately Timothy was a patient child from the very beginning.

The third year of seminary is designed to be an internship year. Thus in August 1964, with our mobile home rented to another seminary family for the year, Jean, year-old Timothy, and I found ourselves heading to Millard, Nebraska, a growing suburb of Omaha. We moved into the "old" parsonage located next to the church, and I began to learn the practical aspect of pastoral ministry. Obvious from the beginning was that we were located in the flight path of jets taking off from the SAC Air Force Base. We gradually adjusted to the unaccustomed noise and to living in a much larger home than the mobile home in which we had been living.

My basic internship duties involved the usual hospital visits, committee meetings, and learning how to deliver a sermon. Like many first time preachers, I initially found myself relying on a written transcript of what I wanted to say. Finding that unacceptable, I then thought that memorizing would be the answer. Not true. The next time under the guidance of Pastor Ihrig I made a few notes concerning what I wanted to say and headed to the pulpit with a prayer for the Holy Spirit to guide me. This seemed to be the most successful method and is the method I have used since. Most of my time during my internship, however, was spent making calls to the unchurched in the Millard area. Since most of the people worked, most of the calls were made during the evening hours. It meant that I had many long days. Meanwhile Jean was busy caring for Tim, spending some days at school as a substitute teacher, and making friends in the congregation.

Soon the internship year ended, and we found ourselves heading back to Dubuque and the seminary. We left with our original possessions, many fine memories, gifts from the congregation and choir, additional possessions we had purchased, and an additional car. We rented a van, hitched the little Anglia we had driven to Millard behind, and drove both the van and our "new" (year-old) Dodge Dart across Iowa back to the Ace Trailer Court. There we, with the aid of my brother Adolf, quickly unloaded the van, and returned immediately to Omaha so that we would arrive within the 24 hour time period of the rental agreement. Tired and sleep deprived, we drove back to Dubuque to begin my final year of study.

Despite our whirlwind return to Dubuque, my last year in seminary was more relaxing and enjoyable than I had previously encountered. This was due largely to the fact that Jean was teaching full time, thanks to a temporary teaching certificate. This meant that I was able to attend class in the morning, pick Tim up from the baby sitter, enjoy and care for him in the afternoon, and study while he napped and played. I did not have to fill my evenings and weekends with the myriad odd jobs that had previously kept us going financially. I did, as is typical of seniors, fill in on Sundays when area churches were in need of a pastor, and other than the first Sunday when the directions to the church and my understanding of them did not match, I was never late.

Seminary graduation came in the spring of 1966, and, except for one class, I was done with my seminary education. We moved to St. Donatus, and I began serving St. John's Lutheran Church in St. Donatus and St. Paul Lutheran Church in La Motte as a student pastor. I finished the class that fall and received my official call to the ministry after I got my diploma in December. My ordination took place at St. Paul Lutheran Church, Conger, Minnesota, on January 8, 1967. Dr. William Streng, a Wartburg Seminary professor, and my father-in-law, Rev. G. D. A. Engelhardt, participated in my ordination service. In February 1967, in the midst of a severe snowstorm, I was installed as full time pastor at St. Donatus and La Motte. As Grandfather had wished for me, I had an education I had taken with me to my place of employment, and I was using my God-given talents to serve others.

The road from Bessarabia to St. Donatus was long, and at times, difficult. Would I have planned my life this way, or could I even have imagined the way it would turn out while I was a child in Germany? Certainly not. But I have no doubt that the hand of the Lord was at work. Without the Russian threat in Bessarabia, my family would have remained there, and I would have followed in my father's footsteps and become a blacksmith. Even my father's death brought us closer to my grandparents, and without my grandfather's urging we probably would never have come to the United States. The many doors the Lord opened (and closed) for me that led eventually to St. Donatus and La Motte and my ministry as a pastor are far too many to count. There is no doubt in my mind that I was guided and protected every step of the way then and each and every day since. His grace has indeed been sufficient. Praise be to God!

Horst and Jean's wedding, St. John's Lutheran Church Preston, IA
1962

Horst's graduation from Wartburg Theological Seminary, Dubuque,
Iowa.1966

Ordination for ministry in the Lutheran Church Jean, Timothy, and Horst at St. Paul Lutheran Church, Conger, Minnesota. January 8, 1967

AFTERWORD

I spent three years at St. Donatus and La Motte. During my third year there in 1969, I accepted a call from Immanuel Lutheran Church in Independence, Iowa. That school year Jean commuted to Wartburg College in Waverly, Iowa, graduating in August 1970. She began teaching half time that fall.

At Independence I experienced clinical pastoral ministry by filling in at the state mental health center. This ministry appealed to me, and after five years I resigned my call so that I could pursue further education. This would enable me to work in a clinical setting, probably as a hospital chaplain. As Jean was teaching full time, she took again the role of "bread winner."

I took three months of study at the mental health center in Independence, followed by another fifteen months at St. Luke Methodist Hospital in Cedar Rapids. Commuting to Cedar Rapids became a problem during the winter snows, so we moved to Cedar

Rapids in January of 1976. I had received my endorsement for ministry in a clinical setting and accepted an opportunity to do marriage counseling for the Family Counseling Service in Cedar Rapids as well as serving as a hospital chaplain at St. Luke. This I did until I accepted a position as hospital chaplain at Jane Lamb Memorial Hospital in Clinton beginning in January 1978.

The rest of my career I spent as a chaplain in Jane Lamb Hospital in Clinton. In 1989 Jane Lamb merged with Mercy Medical Center, and they became my employer. I retired from full time ministry in 2003. Jean retired two years earlier after teaching thirty years in the public schools of Iowa. We continue to live in Clinton most of the year but spend a part of the winter in sunny Arizona. We joyfully celebrated fifty years of marriage with family and friends in June of 2012.

Our second son, Nathan, joined the family four years after our first son, Tim. They have grown into wonderfully intelligent, capable, caring men. Grandfather would have approved their educational choices and their advanced degrees, which enable them to serve others in the health care field. Both have lovely, intelligent wives, who also work in health care. They have favored us with six grandchildren and two great-grandchildren.

My mother continued to live in Minnesota until her death in 2002 at the age of 88. We saw her as often as we were able, and we spoke at length by phone each week. These phone conversations were always in German. She returned to Germany to visit relatives twice. She went with Elmire in 1965 and in 1990 with Jean and me. In 2001 all her children, grandchildren, and great-grandchildren gathered to recognize her fifty years of life in the United States. How pleased she was to be honored in this way and to joyfully celebrate with everyone the family we had become.

My brother Fritz, often called Fred in America, lived and worked in southern Minnesota and northern Iowa until his retirement, when he and his wife, Rose, moved to Oklahoma; after her death he relocated to Florida. They were blessed with two daughters, Rita and Mary, and three grandchildren. My sister, Elmire, trained and worked as a beautician until her marriage. She and her husband, Albert, lived in Albert Lea and raised their two daughters there. Analynn and Adele brought two grandchildren and three step-grandchildren into the family. My brother, Adolf, attended Waldorf Junior College in Forest City, Iowa. He worked in Albert Lea, and after he married and moved to Clinton, he worked in Fulton, Illinois. He and his wife, Janet, have three daughters, Deanna, Dionne, and Doreen; four living grandchildren; and one great-grandchild.

Though Grandfather did not come to the United States, he kept track of the family through correspondence and our visits to Germany. He continued to pray for us until his death in Gyhum in 1973. I think he was pleased, and perhaps a bit proud, of his progeny and the way things turned out. Thanks be to God and His all-sufficient grace.

Adele Hehr in traditional Romanisch attire. c.1990

Adele Hehr's grave marker, Albert Lea, Minnesota. 2003

The Hehr Family
Horst and Jean with their children, grandchildren, and great-grandchildren
Zion Lutheran Church, Clinton, Iowa.
October 12, 2014

APPENDIX

FAMILY ROOTS IN BESSARABIA

Beginning in 1763 Catherine the Great of Russia issued the first of a series of invitations to farmers and skilled laborers to come to Russia. They were promised fertile land, religious freedom, and military exemptions if they would settle and populate areas which were unpopulated or had been devastated by war.

In 1812 another invitation came from Tsar Alexander I, grandson of Catherine, who invited Germans to settle in west Russia. The call was to settle Bessarabia, which had just been acquired in 1812 from the Ottoman Empire at the end of the Russo-Turkish War. It lay in Moldavia between the Prut River to the west and the Dniester River to the east, north of the Black Sea. It was the westernmost province in Russia. The western part of Moldavia is now part of Romania, the eastern part belongs to The Republic of Moldova, and the north and southeastern parts are territories of Ukraine. Alexander's invitation was primarily to the Germans who had migrated to the Warsaw Duchy after the region had been annexed by Prussia in the first partition of Poland in 1772. Conditions there had deteriorated and many found the invitation appealing. Germans from southwest Germany in the Württemberg region also responded to the call to Bessarabia. Approximately 9000 Germans migrated to Bessarabia between 1814 and 1842. They established 25 mother colonies, which grew to more than 150 communities during the 125 years of German colonization of Bessarabia.

(ualberta.ca/~german/PAA/Bessarabians)

My German ancestors, both on my mother's and my father's sides, answered the call to Bessarabia. They apparently were from the group living in the Prussian area of the former Poland, because records show two of my great-grandfathers were born there – Johann Tetzlaff, in 1802, and Michael Hehr, in 1804. Bessarabia is located to the south and east of there, but the Carpathian Mountains stood in the path of a direct route. Hence, when my ancestors decided to accept the invitation to resettle in Bessarabia, they took all their belongings including horses, cattle, sheep, goats, hogs and other livestock and headed north to the Baltic Sea and then east until they got past the Carpathians before they went south to Bessarabia. The end of this arduous, time-consuming journey came for my father's family, the Hehrs, in Alt-Posttal, which was colonized in 1823. My mother's family, the Tetzlaffs, settled in Tarutino, which was about four miles northeast of Alt-Posttal and about 65 miles north of the Black Sea.

Catherine invited the Germans to come to Russia purely for economic reasons. Since she, too, was German, she knew that the skills of the German farmers and workers could help the struggling Russian economy to recover. Alexander's invitation to settle Bessarabia was done for the same reason. Bessarabia was located in a very fertile region -- so fertile, it was reported, that the soil did not need to be augmented with animal waste products, as was the usual practice, so they were dried and used for fuel. Not only was the soil fertile and productive, so were the German immigrants. The 9,000 original immigrants had increased to 25,000 by 1842, to 33,000 by 1861, to 79,000 by 1919 – almost a ten-fold increase in 100 years. (ualberta.ca/~german/PAA/Bessarabians)

My great-grandfather, Michael Hehr, was not a farmer. He was a master blacksmith. His son David also became a master blacksmith, as did my father, Johann. This profession was in great demand, for there were many farm implements to be repaired, scores of horses to be shod, and wagons to be built and sold. And later, of course, there were tractors and other machinery to be repaired. It is not surprising, therefore, that my father usually had two journeymen and three or more apprentices working for him.

In addition to the blacksmith shop where my father worked, the family holdings also included the buildings of the home place - the original house and other outbuildings, where the cows, horses, hogs, sheep, and goats were sheltered and supplies were stored – and some neighboring land. There were vegetable and flower gardens, grasslands, forestland, land for cultivation, a vineyard, and cemetery plots.

As was customary, more than one generation of Hehrs lived in the original Alt-Posttal house during this time - my immediate family, my grandparents, and three of my father's younger unmarried sisters. All contributed to making life run smoothly by preparing meals, doing laundry and other chores, and caring for my older brother Friedrich, my younger sister Elmire, and me. Even the apprentices carried water for the kitchen from the well. My father's younger brothers were working elsewhere in the region, also as blacksmiths.

Daily life for my family continued fairly normally despite the political changes that had occurred in Bessarabia. Over time the promises given by Catherine and Alexander had eroded away. When the exemption from military service was lifted in 1874, many

Germans left Bessarabia, mostly for North America. The outbreak of WW I brought the loss of even more German freedoms and of Germans themselves, including my father's uncles and their families, who emigrated from Bessarabia to Canada. German schools were closed, and German church services and German newspapers were banned. Laws were passed which would enable the government to take the land and send the landholders to Siberia. Fortunately this was averted because of the severe winter and the Bolshevik Revolution in 1917. (ualberta.ca/~german/PAA/Bessarabians) When independence from Russia was granted after WW I, Bessarabia voted to unite with Romania, although Russia never recognized this union. (britannica.com/EBchecked/topic/63021/Bessarabia) The laws concerning the loss of land and the Siberian exile were repealed when the allegiance with Romania occurred. German schools were allowed to reopen, and church services were again allowed in the German language. Eventually even church schools were allowed. By the 1930's German culture and economic prosperity were again thriving in Bessarabia though some of the things promised to the original settlers no longer existed. (ualberta.ca/~german/PAA /Bessarabians)

Things were not, however, as rosy as they seemed. With the Bolshevik Revolution many changes came to Russia including the formation of the Soviet Union. First came the Black party, followed by the Communist party and its idolatrous ideology. The Bessarabians, though currently united with Romania, were fully aware that the Soviet government had never recognized their union and that the creep of Communism across the Soviet Union was likely to present itself at their door in the near future.

The stage was set for confrontation. For over one hundred years the Bessarabian Germans had successfully maintained their culture, language and religion, and Communism was a very real threat to all that had been so diligently preserved. My father, who served as lay minister on many occasions when our pastor, Rev. Dr. Haase, could not reach all five of his churches on a given Sunday, keenly felt the threat. When the pastor could not be in Alt-Posttal, my father would lead the worship service and give the reading, the *Lesung,* in his place. During the week, the church had Bible study, *Versammlung,* which my father led. His siblings, gifted in playing stringed instruments and in singing, made it a festive and spiritually growing experience for the many who faithfully attended.

Because they owed their allegiance to Jesus Christ, my father and his family would never yield to the Communist ideology, which demands allegiance only to the Communist state, ultimately the Communist leader himself, no one else. In the Soviet Union each person was equal, each owning everything, and thereby each owning nothing. Responsibility for everything is impossible, so things were left undone, uncared for, unattended. Property was soon collapsing into uselessness, and the work ethic diminished to where one was given a livelihood whether or not work was done. Eventually, however, when knowledge of such sloth would reach Moscow, the hammer would come down hard, and many a worker literally was forced to work himself into sickness, complete disability, or even death. Labor camps sprang up where these slothful workers and political prisoners met their premature death, some even by starvation.

The Communist Party was meant to replace God. From the Communist viewpoint, the rationale was simply not to believe in a god whom you cannot see. When the tenants of Communism were followed, there was no such thing as sin. Also ruled out was the concept of an afterlife. With these rubbed out, the sacrifice for sin given by Jesus Christ on Calvary and His resurrection were not needed. Since my father and mother were devout, pious Christians, they could not embrace, or even condone, the beliefs of Communism. To my parents Communism was idolatry.

In the meantime Hitler became the absolute ruler of Germany, allied Germany with Austria, conducted massive attacks on German

Jews, and took control of Czechoslovakia. He then, in the fall of 1939, followed closely by Russia, invaded and divided the land of the humble and defensively unprepared people of Poland, which had been re-established after WW I. Hitler gloried in the rapid entrances he made with his *blitzkrieg*, lightning warfare. He convinced Stalin that the thousands of Bessarabians of German descent, who still spoke German, should now settle this newly claimed land in Poland in Germany's behalf. Under the terms of the Hitler-Stalin Pact, they would be able to take what food, furniture, or implements they could carry, but they would not be paid for their land or other accumulated wealth. (ualberta.ca/~german/PAA/Bessarabians) My family did not know of this Hitler-Stalin Pact until some years later. What my father and the other Bessarabian Germans did know was that if they stayed in Bessarabia, their refusal to yield to Communism would unalterably change their life. They would be forced to leave the homes and farms their ancestors had established four generations earlier. Their traditional family structure would be wiped out under Communist rule, and their families would be divided and sent to collective farms, labor camps, and boarding schools. They would no longer be able to worship openly and would be forced to renounce God, whom they believed and trusted for their daily sustenance and salvation from sin.

Their faith in the true and living God, the family life they knew, and the value of all their property accumulated for the past four generations - flower gardens, vegetable gardens, vineyards, fields, forests, cattle, goats, sheep, bees, and, yes, the flourishing blacksmith business - were now most painfully and carefully weighed and measured. Could they remain faithful to the one true God of the Bible and not forsake all that they possessed? What would their life be like under Communism and its interpretation of family, theology, and socialization of all property? What was the real cost of keeping their concept of family, theology, and stewardship of land and possessions?

After much prayer, soul searching, and faith confirmations, my parents, Johann and Adele Hehr, followed what they had known from the beginning was their only real choice and refused to live under Communism. As a result they and the others who made a similar decision were required to leave Alt-Posttal.

Grandfather Eduard Tetzlaff, born August 4, 1887.

Eduard Tetzlaff as a young man.

Grandmother Maria Elisabeth Tetzlaff, *nee* Strohschein,
born August 28, 1892.

Maria Tetzlaff with daughter Adele, Horst's mother.

Johann and Adele Hehr, October 22, 1937, Tarutino, Bessarabia.

Tetzlaff sisters, Adele (Hehr) and Klara (Trautwein). 1937.

Johann Hehr in Alt-Posttal, Bessarabia.

Dr. Daniel Haase, pastor of Tarutino and Alt-Posttal Lutheran
Churches, who baptized Horst and Elmire.

Horst's grandparents Dorthea, *nee* Anhorn, born June 15, 1879, and David Hehr, born December 19, 1875, on their 60th wedding anniversary. Markgröningen, Germany, November 8, 1961

Home built in 1921 by Eduard Tetzlaff in Tarutino, Besserabia. Johann, Elfriede, and Nelly Tetzlaff were born here.

55125070R00096

Made in the USA
Lexington, KY
11 September 2016